WHOA!

Slow Down and Ponder a Life of
Wholeness, Health, Openness and Action

Leta Miller

ISBN: 1973704188
ISBN-13: 978-1973704188

DEDICATION

This book is dedicated to Q, whose infinite and persistent nudging
finally convinced me to start writing again.

~~~~~~~~~~~~~~~~

"You are always with me, and everything I have is yours." Luke 15:31

"Give the opportunity you have been given the respect that it is due."
Rolf Gates and Katrina Kenison

CONTENTS

About the Artwork i

Introduction 3

How to Use This Book 3

What Are We Seeking 4

Infinite Possibilities 6

Happiness 8

Earth Is the Party Planet 10

Stop Apologizing for Your Existence 12

Should & Shouldn't 14

Be Gentle 16

My Bear and My Blankie 18

What is Your Social Set Point? 20

Win List 22

Spirituality & Religion 24

Trusting the Inner Guidance 26

Out of Synch 28

Life Is Working 30

Letting Go 32

Flexibility 34

Commitments 36

From the Outside Looking In 38

One Day at a Time 40

Einstein Time 42

A Crappy Mood 44

CWO Moments 46

Curiosity 48

If I Knew Then What I Know Now 50

Life by Bubba 52

Nothing's Impossible 54

Your God, My God 56

Perfectionism 58

Judgment 60

The Great Waterslide Debate 62

Non-Harming 64

Words Matter 66

Practice 68

Choices 70

Contentment 72

Never Waste a Good Trigger 74

"Cover Me Up!" 76

Rent-Free Living 78

Bacon & Butter 80

Personal Management Team 82

Pay Attention 84

Resiliency 86

Ken, My Greatest Teacher 88

Please Don't 90

Lighten Up 92

Simple Kindness 94

Reframing 96
Lions & Coyotes, Oh My! 98
A Better Idea..100
Change 102
Love or Fear, Which Is It?...104
ADIP 106
Everything Has a Lifespan...108
That Moment When You Know, and It Hurts Like Hell 110
Peaceful vs. Right..112
Five Love Languages...114
What If?...116
Shame..118
Keep Moving 120
35-Minute Heart Opener 122
Personal Manifesto 124
FUN2BEME 126
Be Impeccable with Your Word 128
Slow Medicine 130
Pitch One Thing Every Day...132
Simple Prayer..134
An Ugly Situation 136
Inner Shirley 138
Where You Live...140
Worry...142
Drop the Resistance 144
Don't Make Assumptions 146
Are You a Rule-Follower?...148
Problem with Food?...150
The Love and Sadness of My Mom...............................152
Suffering 154
Do You Really Want to Be Healed?..............................156
It's OK to Not Watch the News......................................158
The Right to Ask..160
Self-Care is Not Optional 162
Autopilot vs. Aware...164
Something to Look Forward To......................................166
Question Everything 168
Salvation 170
You Are Not a Sinner 172
Have To or Get To 174
Bucket List..176
Affirmations..178
Road Trip 180
Baby Steps 182
Heaven 184
They Don't Care 186
"I Love My Life"..188
Doing Nothing 190
Best Day Yet..192
Make Some Art..194
Your Vibration...196
The World in Which You Live.......................................198
Alone Time 200

What's Wrong? What's Right?..202
Don't Take Anything Personally 204
None of Your Business...206
A Good Day to Die...208
Those "Annoying" Bodily Functions 210
Drama...212
The Right to Say Yes or No..214
We Are Never Alone 216
The Big Game...218
Your Own Authority...220
You Are the Answer to Someone's Prayer...222
Your Intimate Relationship with Money 224
A Coach Brings Forth the Best..226
Rudeness, Anger and Peace...228
Bravery...230
The Perfectly Good Airplane 232
Viewing Death as Birth..234
Self-Forgiveness 236
Patience...238
This, Too, Shall Pass..240
Hungry Heart 242
Why Not Smile 244
IMAGE 246
Always Do Your Best 248
Generosity...250
Good or Bad..252
Forgiveness of Others 254
Our Innate Ability to Heal 256
Honoring a Place of Grace...258
Put Down the Phone 260
Completion..262
You Are It 264
What's Next 266

About the Author 268

ABOUT THE ARTWORK

The coloring opportunities throughout the book are
original Zentangle© drawings by the author.
The cover photo is by the author.
The photo of the author is by Paul Hardin.

Introduction

Take a deep breath. Take another, and another. Doesn't it feel good, to be still for just a moment? To take a short time-out? To collect your thoughts? This book invites you to do quite a bit of that, and to enjoy the good feeling of slowing down and being aware in this moment.

You get to learn a whole lot about your magnificent self, and yes, you are magnificent. No matter what the state of your life right now, please know that there is nothing about you that needs to be "fixed." You are not broken or flawed in any way. We are all continually evolving—that's what life is about. We learn and we grow. It's a great adventure, and this book is designed to support your journey.

This book is the result of the wisdom gained in six-plus decades of living. My life has included both full-time and part-time employment, over 30 years of marriage, raising two sons, changing careers, addiction and recovery. I love my life. It is my honor and joy to share what has helped to make my life loveable, supporting you in creating a life you love.

How to Use This Book

There are 122 "ponder sets" in this book, with an occasional short story along the way. Take your time as you consider each subject. My idea in creating this is that you spend three days per topic, taking a year to explore your own magnificent self. Some will require more in-depth exploration; others may not be of interest. Feel free to jump around or go through in a linear fashion. Use the book according to your own inner guidance.

The writings are designated as relating to one or more of four general categories: Wholeness, Health, Openness and Action (hence the title, WHOA!). These four elements are vital to a vibrant, rich life. Wholeness topics look at our true nature as spiritual beings. Health topics address being able to do all you want to do in life. Openness refers to being receptive to all life has to offer. Action topics take your beliefs, dreams and aspirations and make them real.

There is plenty of space with each writing to record your thoughts and experiences. There are spots to doodle and pictures to color. Doodling and coloring loosen the mind to roam freely, which can be very enlightening.

Approach this adventure with an attitude of play. This is your book, your journal, your journey, your life. Slow down and enjoy it!

"If you don't understand yourself, you don't understand anybody else." Nikki Giovanni

What Are We Seeking (W)

Each of us ultimately wants to feel good about the person he is and the life that she is living. Everywhere we go, in every experience, we are the common denominator. We are always in our own heads. We are our own worst critics. We tend to be dreadfully susceptible to the negative opinions of others and often let their positive reinforcement drift away.

I have been in situations wherein I could have behaved differently. I have not done things that I could have done, for my own or someone else's benefit. With these characteristics I am virtually indistinguishable from every other being on the planet. All these things are simply situations which bring us information. If the results are not pleasing, and we are smart, we won't repeat the unpleasant experience. Therein lies the opportunity to feel good.

Serenity is priceless. It does not come from doing or having. It only comes from being comfortable with who we are, from our inner being. It does not come from being perfect. It is the result of accepting ourselves just as we are and viewing life as a learning experience filled with choices which we are fully capable of making.

"When you understand that what most people really, really want is simply to feel good about themselves, and when you realize that with just a few well-chosen words you can help virtually anyone on the planet instantly achieve this, you begin to realize just how simple life is, how powerful you are, and that love is the key." Mike Dooley

To Ponder: What have I done that I could have done differently? What have I not done that I could have done? Can I release these things and forgive myself, loving myself a bit more?

Ponderings

Infinite Possibilities (O)

Any given moment, the now is all we ever have. We cannot hold onto the past or the future. Certainly we can worry or stress over each of those. While we may have photos of past events, in truth they are gone, nothing more than a thought, a fondly-held (or not) memory. Regarding the future, with infinite possibilities at our command, we are taking on a monumental task trying to control those possibilities in advance. We are asking for distress when we do this.

Why don't we recognize the infinite possibilities in each moment? We are conditioned by life to do what we have always done. For instance, look at the simple task of driving to work. Most people take the same route day after day. It's a habit, something that we rarely consider consciously. In fact, there are an unlimited number of ways to get there. We just don't take advantage of that fact due to gas prices or time constraints or simple habit. We notice other possibilities when life throws an accident or a highway repair project into our usual route.

While the route to work we choose may not seem to be of great cosmic significance, what is significant is the pattern. It is the lack of recognition of choices that leads us to stay in a job or profession that we despise for decades or a lifetime, to stay mired in addiction, to live by the belief that we are meant to suffer and to settle for less than a happy life.

The universe radiates infinity—people, grass, grains of sand, planets, stars, space. Think of the billions of people on the planet, no two exactly alike; in every moment, each one is experiencing something different based on their perception. I live in Kansas where the sky is huge and mostly uncluttered by buildings, mountains and trees. We get to enjoy glorious sunrises and sunsets. No two are ever alike, and in every moment they change. The canvas of the universe is an ever-changing kaleidoscope that is infinitely different in every moment.

One way I like to practice awareness of other possibilities is to do something differently from my habitual routine every day. It may be as simple as operating a spray-bottle with my non-dominant hand. This helps me build awareness of my tendencies to live on autopilot and not recognize the options available to me.

"Once self-awareness dawns in you, the questions you can ask about yourself, about how you think and feel, have no limit. Self-aware questions are the keys that make consciousness expand, and when that happens, the possibilities are infinite." Deepak Chopra

To Ponder: What change can I make today—perform a task in a new way or drive a different route? How did the change go? What can I do differently tomorrow?

Ponderings

Happiness (W)

"There is only one choice, out of the infinity of choices available in every second, that will create happiness for you as well as for those around you. And when you make that one choice, it will result in a form of behavior that is called spontaneous right action. Spontaneous right action is the right action at the right moment. It's the right response to every situation as it happens. It's the action that nourishes you and everyone else who is influenced by that action." Deepak Chopra

There is absolutely nothing outside of us that can make us happy. Happiness is an inside job. It is an internal state of being that comes from experiencing life consciously connected to our inner guidance.

The sports car, the fancy house, the fat checking account, the soul mate—all these things can bring us pleasure, but not happiness. Many times we seek happiness in those outer things as a substitute for the spiritual nourishment we truly need. Drugs, alcohol, food, sex, gambling—all the addictive substances and behaviors are a misguided search for happiness on the outside. The 12-Step programs have been successful in helping millions of people recover from addiction because they turn the focus inward to a personal relationship with a power greater than the addict.

The search for happiness outside us appears to be the easy route because when we look inside, we often don't like what we see. We are our own worst enemies, and there is often plenty to criticize. We should have done that and we didn't; we shouldn't have done this and we did. We feel guilt and shame and frustration and disappointment. We feel unlovable and defective.

We did not come into this earthly form with any of that baggage. We came here as perfect, whole and complete beings, spiritually full and infinitely loved. Those negative feelings we drag around, sometimes for a lifetime, come from outside comparisons and expectations. There is nothing in our essence that demands that we do, be or have more.

Negative personal feelings are like spiritual splinters. They irritate and fester. We try to ignore them, or cover them up with outer "Band-Aids" like the sports car or fancy house. It is essential that we remove these splinters which are infecting us. We are designed to be happy and to enjoy this earthly adventure.

The nearly universal answer parents give to the question "what do you want for your children?" is that they want them to be happy. How do they learn that if parents don't model it for them? Please ponder that very thoughtfully if you are a parent.

"The opportunity to find happiness dances within every moment, beats within every heart, and grooves within every occurrence, situation, and event." Mike Dooley

To Ponder: Is it OK to be happy? Am I happy? If not, why not? What makes me happy?

Ponderings

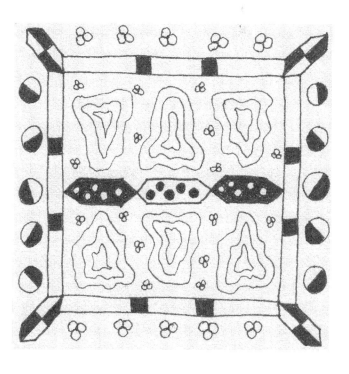

Earth Is the Party Planet (O)

Play with me here for a bit. Your soul, your eternal being, is out of earthly form, enjoying a glorious life on "the other side." Life there is one instant gratification after another. You have eternity, literally forever, to enjoy this and nothing you do can change this fact. You develop a hankering for an adventure, a break in the eternally perfect routine. Someone suggests the "earth game" to you.

In the earth game, you can choose to experience literally anything you want to experience (infinite possibilities, you see). Given that you have eternity, even a lengthy earth game is really just a tiny blip in time.

You go through the process of leaving the other side and taking on a human form. You remember at least for a time where you came from and what you are, a limitless eternal being. You play and explore and learn to make noise to get your needs met. It seems to be a pretty fun game until you start to encounter resistance. There are other game players here who say "no" and impose limitations on you.

Gradually, in order to fit in with the more experienced earth game players, you adapt to their rules and regulations. The freedom, ease and delight of the other side becomes a vague memory. The other players may even be able to convince you that the earth game is all there is—that you are just a body meant to suffer here, then die.

But wait! There is something inside you that <u>knows</u> otherwise. You know that you are more than what the other players are telling you; that somewhere along the way you came here to play, for a break in the eternal sameness. Listening within to the voice that knows the truth is the key. All those other earth game players are suffering and frustrated *because* they are looking outside themselves for the key to enjoying life here on earth.

Once you remember who you are, an eternal, powerful and creative being with infinite possibilities, wow! Earth really does become your playground. You know that your true self can never be destroyed. You delight in bringing this news to other players. Any adventure is possible. The results don't actually matter, as it is the experience itself that is important, regardless of how other players may choose to judge your efforts.

"Each one of us decides to incarnate upon this planet at a particular point in time and space. We have chosen to come here to learn a particular lesson that will advance us upon our spiritual, evolutionary pathway." Louise L. Hay

To Ponder: Is this story truly whacked-out, or does it tug at my heartstrings a bit? Can I open my mind enough to play with this story? How would my life change if I believed this description of life on earth to be true?

Ponderings

Stop Apologizing for Your Existence (A)

The first time I say this title phrase to anyone, I can nearly guarantee a blank look in return. I did the same thing when I first heard this in yoga training with Ana Forrest. The blank looks result from the fact that this behavior is so ingrained, it's completely unconscious. We don't even know we are doing it.

One example of this behavior is saying "sorry" frequently, for instance, "I'm sorry, but would you help me with this?" This says right up front that you think you're a bother to someone. It fairly screams lack of confidence. Use of "sorry" like this devalues the use of "I'm sorry" when you truly mean it in apology.

Here's another example. One day at the gym, upon returning to my locker after showering, I found another woman using the locker next to mine, getting dressed. Her back was to me. I was in no hurry and waited silently nearby so that she could finish unhurried. After a few minutes, she turned around and saw me waiting. She freaked and said, "Am I in your way?" I replied, "No, take your time, I'm in no hurry." She didn't hear me. She started apologizing profusely, collected all her stuff (even though she wasn't completely dressed), and moved everything elsewhere. She apologized profusely for her presence in "my" space, but there was no problem with her being there in the first place.

Because this behavior is so unconscious, it's a bit of a challenge to even notice you're engaging in it. Pay attention to your use of "sorry," "excuse me," "I hate to bother you but," and so on. You are here on Playground Earth for a reason, so stop apologizing for yourself.

"I'm sorry if I behaved in a way that makes you think I should apologize but I won't because I know I didn't do anything wrong." Anonymous

To Ponder: As I look at a typical day, when do/did I use the trigger words or phrases mentioned above? Describe the circumstance. Was I apologizing for my existence? How can I change my words to behave more confidently in such situations?

Ponderings

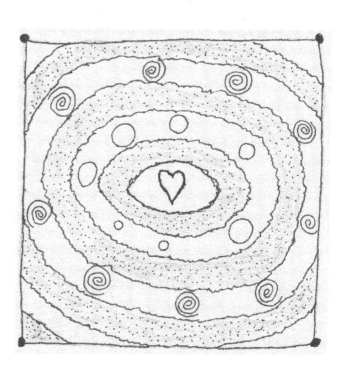

Should & Shouldn't (A)

I can't stress strongly enough what "red flag" personal danger words these two are. Watching out for just these two words will offer you a huge leap forward in self-awareness, understanding and care. Most likely they will be easy to find on any given day.

They are indicators of a breakdown in your integrity, not following your heart or inner guidance.

Let's look first at the instance of hearing these words from others. If someone is telling you that you should or shouldn't do something, she is trying to get you to behave the way that she wants you to, not necessarily what you want. If it takes convincing from someone else, you can be fairly certain you are going against your inner knowing. "You should serve on that committee." "You shouldn't buy that dress, it's too expensive." Should and shouldn't directed at you by someone else is a controlling maneuver.

Then there is the unending replay of should and shouldn't inside our own heads. We imagine the voice of society or family or spouse or some other influential entity telling us what we should or shouldn't do, be or have. It's so important when faced with a choice to consider what <u>feels</u> good and right to you, and go with that, no matter what should or shouldn't is yelling for your attention. If you've ever gone with the should option over your gut-feel choice (who hasn't?), you know that the results can be exceedingly unpleasant, because you've put yourself somewhere you do not want to be.

Should and shouldn't are powerful weapons in our society. It's not easy to stick with one's inner guidance and go against the overly-offered advice of others. It's a practice, like all of life. As we record one small victory at a time, our ability to disregard should and shouldn't gets stronger.

"Just because you can doesn't mean you should." Sherrilyn Kenyon

To Ponder: As I go through the day, when do I hear should and shouldn't, either from another or in my own head? What was it in reference to? If I made a choice, what did I decide? How did that feel?

Ponderings

Be Gentle (H)

It seems that gentleness gets a bad rap in our hard-driving, results-oriented culture. It also seems that everyone loves touches of gentleness, literal or figurative.

Gentleness is a practice, and it starts with your own self. This book is an adventure of self-exploration. It is grounded in the simple truth that each human being is magnificent, and this earthly journey is one of discovery, not of trials and suffering. Life is challenging enough without dragging ourselves down with the idea that we are broken or fault-filled and need to be repaired. There is nothing to fix.

If there's nothing wrong with us, why bother with this book or the multitude like it? It's about self-knowing, the most powerful knowledge there is, and about making conscious choices. A favorite saying used by Ana Forrest (my yoga teacher) is "evolve or die." We continue to learn, grow and expand if we want to experience a full life, otherwise we do wither and die.

Gentleness comes into play when we allow ourselves to move at our own pace, to our own rhythm in life, not forced or rushed by outer influences. As spiritual teacher Edwene Gaines says, "We all do things we wouldn't want to tell to our grandmothers." We slip up, we get back on track, over and over. We can learn to be gentle with ourselves in the process. It makes getting back on track so much easier.

As we learn to offer ourselves the gift of gentleness, it expands from us out into the world. We learn to treat other humans, all creatures and our extraordinary planet with a gentle, loving, relaxed and accepting attitude. A world of peace starts with each of us being gentle with our magnificent selves.

"Nothing is so strong as gentleness, nothing so gentle as real strength." Saint Francis de Sales

To Ponder: In what ways am I not so gentle with myself? What conscious choices can I make to be more gentle? How could the practice of gentleness bring more ease into my life?

Ponderings

My Bear and My Blankie

I have a bear and his name is Ted. He's a koala bear, actually. He is a constant reminder of the love of my late sister-in-law, Mary Ellen. He's been steadfastly watching over me for about 50 years.

You may have heard the phrase "defining moment." That's when something so big happens, it changes the course of your life. If you ponder a bit, you'll come up with one or more in your own life.

My defining moment relevant to this story was my mother burning my beloved blanket when I was around age 12. I had thwarted her two previous attempts at disposal via trash. Ken and Mary Ellen had been married a couple of years, their son Kevin was here, possibly daughter Cheryl. I was actively helping Mary Ellen with the children because my brother, Ken, lying on the couch and yelling, was no help at all.

Mary Ellen, God bless her sweet soul, was the only one who recognized what a trauma the blanket-burning was for me, and she bought me Ted Bear as a "replacement" for my blanket.

Mary Ellen became my "go-to" person. At that young age, I felt that she was the only person in my daily life that I could trust. After all, if you can't trust your mom, who can you trust?!?!

I truly don't know if I'd have made it through my teen years without Mary Ellen. Having four children over a seven-year span, she needed plenty of help, and I adored my nephew and three nieces. Helping her made me feel useful and gave me a sense of value, and it gave me lots of time with the one person I trusted and loved dearly. I learned mothering from her, so I knew that I could do it when my turn came. Even though she didn't spend a lot of time with my sons, she has had, and continues to have, a large effect on their lives, too. Mary Ellen was a very special person, and I am one incredibly blessed woman to have had her powerful love in my life.

A few years ago, working with my spiritual coach, I realized that if I wanted to, I could once again have a "blankie." So what if I'm an adult. That very day I went out and purchased one of the same color as the original, that mint green "we don't know if the baby is a boy or girl" safe color. It is not the same fabric, but has the same silky binding that my original had. It's on my lap right now as I write this. It is comforting to me. It feels like love to me. It makes me smile. You, too, can have a blankie if you would like.

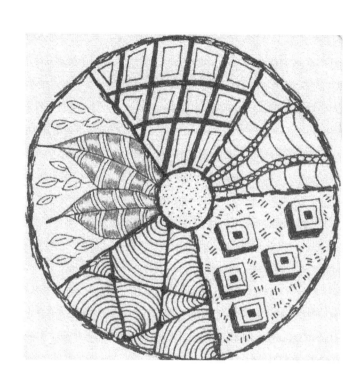

What is Your Social Set Point? (H)

The idea of a set point in terms of social behavior is that we tend to be more introverted or more extroverted, and we tend to stay that way our whole life. No one is completely one way or the other, but each of us has a tendency to dwell toward one end of the social-interaction spectrum.

An introvert needs to feel safe in the space she is in and with the surrounding people. If this is not the case, the introvert tends to feel quite drained by the social interaction. Introverts may be considered less friendly than extroverts, but this is not the case. Introverts simply tend to be more cautious and deliberate in social interactions.

This writing is in support of the world's introverts. Somewhere along the way, being an introvert got a bad rap, and it seems introverts got the idea that they shouldn't be that way, that they should get out there and be extroverts. So developed yet another way for folks to feel poorly about themselves. I write this from personal experience.

I recently joined a group that is hugely in support of being who you are, and there are lots of introverts in the group. I had been feeling that I had overcome some of my introverted tendencies over the years, like that was a worthwhile fix-myself mission. In this group, and in all my life now, I give myself permission to be an introvert. I've said for decades that I could easily be a hermit. I'm good with that. I like my own company. I enjoy others, too, in limited doses. Then I need alone time. It's my set point, and I'm happy with it.

I encourage you to stand strong and be who you are. Enjoy your social set point. Be as introverted as you care to be. It's OK. If you are an extrovert, good for you. There's nothing to fix—you are awesome just the way you are!

"A good rule of thumb is that any environment that consistently leaves you feeling bad about who you are is the wrong environment." Laurie Helgoe

"I don't hate people, I just feel better when they aren't around." Charles Bukowski

To Ponder: What is my social set point? Have I ever felt like I should be different from the way I am? What are the advantages of my personal set point?

Ponderings

Win List (A)

The Win List is a tool that I first encountered in the book, "Inspired and Unstoppable," by Tama Kieves. The idea is to note briefly each day your wins or successes for the day. You also include instances of synchronicity, where you've recognized something bigger than yourself supporting you in some way, such as unexpected income. It's a personal list, so a win for you may not be a win for me. There's no wrong way to do a Win List (other than not doing one).

Wins don't have to be earth-shaking or life-changing events, though they can be. Any willingness on my part to do some house-cleaning is a win for me, albeit a somewhat boring one. The idea is to focus on the positives in your life, and as you do so, the number of positives expands. Another important aspect of the Win List is to celebrate the successes, which folks in general are woefully remiss in doing on a regular basis.

My Win List has been going strong for several years. I keep it in Google Drive so that I have ready access to it from my phone or laptops. I keep it updated even when I'm on vacation. It's typically less than a five minute task. Another great service the Win List provides is the opportunity for "the year in review." I did this recently at a year-end and discovered even more to celebrate than I initially remembered. Celebrating the year just completed is a great way to move into the next year. It's powerful momentum.

"It's the game of life. Do I win or do I lose? One day they're gonna shut the game down. I gotta have as much fun and go around the board as many times as I can before it's my turn to leave." Tupac Shakur

To Ponder: Start a Win List. Update daily. Celebrate successes, no matter the size.

Ponderings

Spirituality & Religion (W)

I was raised in a particularly stern and strict religion. I thought that was the way to live a faith-based, useful life until I encountered spirituality in a 12-step program. I have passed in my lifetime through several religious organizations, even working at a church for a half-dozen years. Ultimately, my belief system has evolved so that I no longer practice any religion. I'm good with that, and I have no worries about my soul for eternity.

Religion often has a hold on people because they've been told they will go to hell if they aren't a "believer," faithfully subscribing to the written and unwritten dogma of that religion. In the next breath, they say "God is love." Those two lines don't synch up for me. Many religions also have the tendency to believe "we are right and they are wrong" about other religions.

On the positive side, participating in a religious organization can provide one with a sense of community. It can also provide a place to be of service. It can be a source of comfort and support. It can provide education relative to living a faith-based life. I have derived all those things from my previous religious experiences.

Spirituality is based in who we are, the universal knowing that we are, every one of us, spiritual beings having a human experience. We are fine just as we are, not broken or flawed or sinful. We are all connected, created of the same stuff. What damages one, damages all. What uplifts one, uplifts all. There is some greater intelligence that has created everything and keeps all of it, including your life and mine, in an orderly flow. We are all equal, and equally loved, within this intelligence. It is possible to have a personal relationship with it.

Religious people can be very spiritual, and spiritual folks can be quite involved in a religion. However, religion is not required to be spiritual. Religion is not required to live a good and useful life. Striving to live well is common sense, no religious dogma or threat of damnation required.

If you participate in a religious community and it serves you, continue to do so. Most importantly, cultivate a rich spiritual life. Expand your knowledge of your true nature, a child of the infinite. Explore the unique and beautiful human you are. Broadening your spiritual knowledge benefits you personally, and blesses the rest of humanity, too.

"I'm doing my best to be mindful about how I'm living: to be kind and patient, and not to impose a bad mood on somebody else. Being mindful is as good a way to be spiritual as anything else." Deirdre O'Kane

To Ponder: Do I actively participate in a religious organization? Does it support my life? What do I do to develop my spiritual awareness? How can I bring more spirituality into my religion?

Ponderings

Trusting the Inner Guidance (W/O/A)

We all have it. Some call it a gut feeling or intuition or inner knowing. It is that permanent connection to the other side we came from, to the infinite source of love and goodness in which we eternally exist. We came into this earthly life completely in touch with this inner knowing. Using it is a skill we can easily rekindle.

This is the "talking to myself" part of us. We are all talking to ourselves all the time, whether or not we are paying attention to the chatter. We are also continually receiving guidance, and living joyfully requires going with that guidance, unfailingly, even when it seems to make no sense. This is definitely a practice.

The best way I have found to practice following my inner guidance is through living spontaneously. (See Chopra's quote under **Happiness**, p. 8.) This is taking the next right action that you <u>want</u> to take, no "should" or "shouldn't" involved. If there is any sense of discomfort about a choice we are making, it is not a spontaneous right action. In each moment, the goal is to be functioning either in a state of enthusiasm, enjoyment or peaceful acceptance. If we are not experiencing one of these three states of being, then it is not spontaneous living. Experiencing discomfort of any sort means there is harm involved in what we are doing, possibly to others, and certainly to ourselves. At the very least, we are limiting our joy.

Another characteristic of spontaneous living is giving up the need to judge circumstances and people. The go-with-the-flow nature of life incorporates the belief that everything in every moment is perfect just the way it is, and there is no need to see it as otherwise.

Living spontaneously makes you happy in the present moment. Adding up many happy moments creates days, weeks, months and years of a happy life. That's what makes this practice so worthwhile.

Here's an example of a "bigger picture" spontaneous choice. I work an intense three-month tax preparation job each year from mid-January to mid-April. With my other part-time work continuing, I end up working about 50 hours a week. While there is definitely enjoyment in the work, this mostly falls into the "peaceful acceptance" category because the job pays extraordinarily well, and it supports my travel habit the rest of the year. Traveling is my favorite thing, and the Universe has provided me an awesome way to do it via the tax job.

"Ultimately spiritual awareness unfolds when you're flexible, when you're spontaneous, when you're detached, when you're easy on yourself and easy on others." Deepak Chopra

To Ponder: How much time do I spend doing tasks because I "should"? What do I <u>want</u> to do? What's keeping me from doing what I want to do?

Ponderings

Out of Synch (A)

How do I know when I am not living spontaneously? I'm tense, anxious, worried about getting stuff done, forcing things to happen, and doing things I don't want to be doing because I should. I am not trusting that I live in a Universe that always works for me. I'm trying to control things that are out of my range. I am easily upset. I'm not happy or content or peaceful.

One of my major things in life that I have done because I should is house-cleaning. As an example of how we unconsciously get locked into patterns—when I was a teenager, it was my responsibility to clean our house, and it had to all be done on Friday or Saturday morning. I couldn't do anything fun until the house-cleaning was done. So when I moved into a home of my own, I went with the "clean it all at once" mentality. GRRRR! Instant crankiness! That also meant that I rarely had the time or interest in doing it, so I was either forcing myself to clean or feeling guilty because I wasn't cleaning. Spontaneous living has conquered cleaning for me. I break the cleaning into manageable units and do small tasks often. That way I have the satisfaction of getting some cleaning done without the torture of doing it all at once. My house is rarely all clean at one time, and I'm OK with that. Think for a moment about a similar "chore" in your life that could be conquered with spontaneous living.

It is a worthwhile exercise in self-examination to look at the issue of whether you believe life is supposed to be one of fun and joy, or one of suffering and trial. Spontaneous living will always lead to fun and joy, and never to suffering.

"The supreme accomplishment is to blur the line between work and play." Arnold J. Toynbee

To Ponder: What is a necessary task that leaves me feeling out of synch with myself, as described above? How can I approach it differently to get it done without sacrificing peace?

Ponderings

Life Is Working (A)

What is life like when you are living by spontaneous right action? You are talking to yourself, continuously asking what the next right choice is, then going with the answer. Your life flows, and somehow everything gets done in an easy and effortless manner. Things simply work out in amazing ways. Rarely does anything upset you. You are happy and content and peaceful. It is this peaceful nature within each one of us that creates peace in our world. So by living in spontaneous right action, we are not only benefiting ourselves, but we are also blessing our world.

The wise person living spontaneously also lives in a constant state of gratitude. What a blessing it is to be content with what you are doing in each moment. The words "should" and "shouldn't" rarely enter your thoughts. There is complete freedom from fear, guilt, shame and judgment. There is no concern over what others think about you, and you have no need to seek the praise of others. You choose how the actions of others affect you. You are a self-contained, complete whole.

You also accept full responsibility for your life experience, feelings, thoughts and actions. After all, when life is this good, you deserve to take credit for it. You don't drag around baggage from the past, such as resentments, addictions and unfinished business. You live and let live, not taking anything personally.

Dreams and goals regularly and consistently become reality. You live in a self-fulfilling state of enjoyment and enthusiasm. A life of enthusiasm and gratitude continually attracts even more bounty. You are setting an inspiring example for others to follow. You don't become attached to results. It's all good.

The practice of living spontaneously is a very worthwhile spiritual exercise.

"The life you have left is a gift. Cherish it. Enjoy it now, to the fullest. Do what matters, now." Anonymous

To Ponder: At least once today—ask myself what I most want to do, listen to my inner knowing and do it. How did it feel to take this action? Keep practicing this.

Ponderings

Letting Go (A)

Spontaneous right action is the anathema of the ego, the part of us that operates on "should." Our egos like to control us and strive to keep us in line by the use of fear. Living spontaneously circumvents the ego by making our intuition the guide of our actions. We live with complete trust in Spirit to direct us for our highest good.

Attachment to outcomes is recognized by all major religions as the root of suffering. One common phrase for attachment is being a control freak. Attachment is the endless search and demand for security, which is hopeless in a world where no form is permanent and change is constant. The only way to inner peace in a world of constant change is to learn to live with uncertainty and flexibility, that is, by detaching from the known. Letting go requires faith in a benevolent power greater than we are, and it especially requires trusting ourselves.

The hallmark of detachment is the freedom to create in the field of infinite possibilities. We don't need to give up our goals and desires. We just need to give up trying to control how those things will come about. The Universe conspires endlessly and infinitely on our behalf, so why limit our options by trying to control the process? Let go, let go, let go.

"Without detachment we are prisoners of helplessness, hopelessness, mundane needs, trivial concerns, quiet desperation, and seriousness — the distinctive features of everyday mediocre existence and poverty consciousness." Deepak Chopra

To Ponder: Which situation(s) or person(s) am I trying to control? How's that working? What would happen if I let go? Can I let go and trust?

Ponderings

Flexibility (A)

Willingness to live spontaneously means we give up the need to control life, people and circumstances. I was, most of my life, a card-carrying control freak, organized to a fault, with my days rigidly planned before I even rolled out of bed in the morning. A sure way to make me irritable was to mess up my day's plans in some way.

As I have come to rely more on my inner guidance to direct the flow of my days, I have learned to enjoy the flexibility. It is wonderful to be free of a rigidly planned schedule and to enjoy the contentment of doing what feels right at any given moment. This practice enables me to follow intuitional nudges and enjoy where they lead me.

One of the rewards of living spontaneously is the removal of "should" from our self-talk vocabulary. Doing something because we should and avoiding something because we should not are in direct opposition to living a contented and spontaneous life. Living under the "should" cloud yields days of forced behavior and resentment. A great deal of personal unhappiness can be traced to the words "should" and "shouldn't."

Flexible living in the moment greatly enhances our relationships. It becomes much easier to take "no" for an answer without taking it personally. We honor the inner guide in others as well as our own, and recognize that their choices truly have nothing to do with us.

Living with a flexible mindset also enables us to learn to be willing to let things slide, to not do a task if it doesn't feel right. This is not to be confused with procrastination. We can tell with practice whether the ego is telling us to procrastinate or our inner guide is offering a "wait on that" message. A thoughtful look at nature reveals an easy, intelligent, comfortable flow in which everything gets accomplished at the appropriate time. We can live that way, too.

"The ability to recognize opportunities and move in new - and sometimes unexpected - directions will benefit you no matter your interests or aspirations." Drew Gilpin Faust

To Ponder: How rigid is my schedule? How can I relax it a bit? How often do I hear "should" or "shouldn't" in my mental chatter? Do one thing today because it feels right in the moment. How did it go? Keep practicing this.

Ponderings

Commitments (A)

It is quite possible to live spontaneously and continue to plan and schedule future events and make commitments. A check-in with our inner guidance will again reveal whether it feels right to make the dental appointment or agree to help with a service project. If it doesn't feel right in the moment to commit to something, it won't feel good to actually have to do it at some later time.

This leads us to an extremely important characteristic of a balanced, happy life—self-trust. This may be one of life's most challenging practices, especially if you were raised in an environment where your thoughts, feelings and expressions were discounted. We know what we know and feel what we feel, and that's all valid. It's certainly a learning process, even with the best of upbringings, to be confident and content to stand in one's choices. We may also have to contend with others' fussing about our choices. You know right away that someone is following their own self-interest if they are telling you what you should or shouldn't do. Don't let those offers of "guidance" dissuade you from your choice.

Self-trust is greatly enhanced when we recognize and celebrate our successes, no matter how small. We tend to overlook them, anxious to move on to the next challenge or task to check off our list. Note how good it feels when you follow your heart and things turn out well. Appreciate the fact that you made a choice and stuck with it.

"It's amazing to allow yourself to dare your own authentic walk in this lifetime, to listen to the love within you more than your fear." Tama Kieves

To Ponder: Am I committed to anything now that I really didn't want to do? Looking back, were there any indications earlier that this didn't feel right? Note those signals. What choice(s) did I make today that turned out well? Celebrate each victory.

Ponderings

From the Outside Looking In (O)

This is the place from which we perceive the lives of others. Unfortunately, we often use this vantage point as our pedestal for judging them and how they choose to live. I liken this to looking through a keyhole in an old-fashioned door. You can only see a tiny bit of the room on the other side. From the outside looking into someone's life, likewise, you can only see a tiny bit of theirs.

Even those who are closest to us, spouse, children, best friend for life, we simply don't completely know them and what they may have "signed up for" in this life. We don't know all the experiences they have had which lead them to make the choices they do.

One of the great challenges I have had in life is letting my 20-something sons learn the life lessons of that decade. I am frequently reminded that life for them is different from when I was in my 20s, that they do not know what I know, and that no amount of my imparting my knowledge is helpful to them. I must simply look in from the outside and love them.

Judging others from our limited perspective is helpful neither to them or ourselves. Edwene Gaines, spiritual teacher and very wise woman, suggests this judgment-disarming tactic. When one is tempted to criticize another, take a breath and simply say, "Isn't that interesting?" It's a gentle reminder to live and let live, that we don't have the almighty ability to see another's situation from the outside looking in.

"Watch out for the joy-stealers: gossip, criticism, complaining, faultfinding, and a negative, judgmental attitude." Joyce Meyer

To Ponder: When I am tempted to judge another? Describe the situation. Is my judgment helpful? How could I be helpful in this situation? Is it really any of my business?

Ponderings

One Day at a Time (A)

For the addictive personality, this idea suggests that we can do for just one day what we most likely cannot do for a whole lifetime. Just for today, we choose not to indulge in the drug of choice, be it alcohol, food, shopping, gambling or whatever.

In the broader perspective, this "one day" is all we have. While we may be carrying around baggage from yesterdays, they are gone. While we may be fretting over upcoming days, they are not yet here. It is in living this one day well that we elevate both the yesterdays and the upcoming days.

We can do several things each day to make this "one day" a satisfying one. We can set the intention first thing in the morning to make this day a good one, and to stay within this one day and not wander off into the past or the future. We can take time to visualize the day as we would like it to be, particularly seeing ourselves as calm, not rushed, smiling, interacting harmoniously with others, and accomplishing what we choose to do that day.

Focusing on today keeps us from getting overwhelmed by future events. When I wander off into fears of the future, I breathe and remind myself, "Right now, all is well." Those of us in the habit of making a to-do list would do well to focus on the moderate amount we can do on this one day, rather than seeking to cram in too much, leading to frustration and burnout.

At the end of the day, we can look over the events of the day and give ourselves a pat on the back for intentions set and accomplished. Also, right then and there, we can recognize events requiring us to forgive ourselves and others and visualize them enfolded in a circle of love and bless them. Having done these things, we don't drag baggage into the new day tomorrow.

"I'm like a recovering perfectionist. For me it's one day at a time." Brene Brown

To Ponder: Take a few moments before starting the day to set an intent and mentally picture a satisfying day. Stop for breathing breaks throughout the day. In the evening, review how the day went. What did I learn about myself and living? Repeat one day at a time.

Ponderings

Einstein Time (O/A)

"For your life to work harmoniously, you need to develop a harmonious relationship with time. Most people have a difficult time balancing all of their priorities. And there is no greater priority than transforming your relationship with time."
Gay Hendricks in "The Big Leap"

Einstein time is based on one simple truth: you create time. Therefore you can create as much as you want. While this may at first seem an absurd idea, think on it. Cavemen didn't have clocks, yet they got done what needed to be done. Time and time-keeping devices are human inventions.

The secret to using Einstein time is being fully present and relaxed in the space you are in, rather than the future (what's gonna happen) or the past (what did happen). And you must take full charge of your own personal time. Drop the idea that time is something outside of you. You are not a victim of time, and the best way to manifest this knowing in life, and a great way to implement Einstein time in your life, is to stop complaining (right now!) about time.

Look at the phrase, "I don't have time for that right now." That's being a victim of time and using it to mask your real sentiment, which is "I don't want to do that right now." Pay attention to the words you use about time. Get honest, taking charge of the time you create.

Mr. Hendricks talks about two general personality types relative to time: the Time Cop and the Time Slacker. The Time Cop (I am one!) is always on time and expects everyone else to be on time, too. The Time Slacker doesn't care about time constraints of any sort. I once bought one son a t-shirt that read, "On time is when I get there." That's a perfect description of the Time Slacker. Folks tend to be one or the other. The key point is that both Cops and Slackers can effectively use Einstein time.

With Einstein time, you get to leave the extremes of your old view of time: either not enough time (stress) or too much time (boredom). You create just the right amount of time, yielding a life of less stress and more creativity because you have time to think. You never feel hurried, get more done in less time, and you feel peaceful and energetic instead of drained. Einstein time works.

"You'll never have enough money to buy all the stuff you don't really need, and you'll never have enough time to do the things you really don't want to do." Gay Hendricks

To Ponder: How often do I complain about time? Feel victimized by time? Remind myself to take ownership of my time, that I create as much as I want. Practice, practice, practice. What am I learning about myself and my relationship to time?

Ponderings

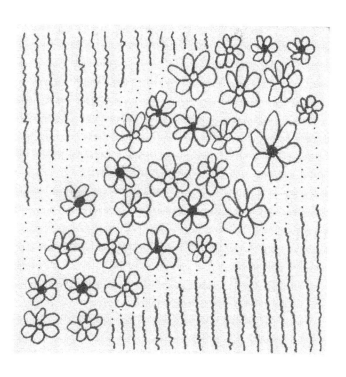

A Crappy Mood (A)

It happens to all of us. The current dose of life, for whatever reason, results in a crappy mood. I feel cranky, out-of-sorts and really not fit to be around others for the time being. I've learned to flow with that feeling, even though it's not as pleasant as a happy mood. I generally choose as much as possible to be away from others. When interactions are required, however, I make a special effort to be polite, so as not to leave any trashy feelings in my wake.

Going with a crappy mood has proven to dissipate it much more quickly than if I try to convince myself that I am not, or should not be, in a crappy mood. Often in an effort to burn off negative energy, I will do an unpleasant task like mowing or cleaning. Since I'm in a bad mood anyway, I may as well do a nasty chore. I accomplish something, which will help lift the funk.

It's also a good idea when I'm in a crappy mood for me to speak as little as possible. There is too strong a tendency to say things which I would regret.

Another thing about a crappy mood—I do not need to be fixed. A crappy mood is a passing thing, not a physical ailment requiring surgery. We would do each other a great service if we would just let each other have the feelings of the moment and not take it personally and not try to fix it. Acceptance is the issue here. Granted, it is easier to accept the joyful feelings, but we came here to this earthly life to experience the full gamut of feelings, so why not simply flow with it? Every feeling passes into another eventually. It is part of the ebb and flow of life.

"Nothing is more annoying than being in a bad mood for no apparent reason and being asked 'what's wrong' over and over again." Anonymous

To Ponder: What is my experience of a crappy mood? Do I allow myself to have negative feelings? How do I behave in a crappy mood? What enables it to pass? How do I react to someone else who is in a crappy mood?

Ponderings

CWO Moments (O)

A glorious fringe benefit of living on our magnificent planet is what I refer to as the completely-wide-open moment. These are moments when all thinking has ceased, and I am so focused in the current moment that I feel "lifted" out of my normal existence. It is a moment so brief and so awesome that I expect it is a remembrance of how life routinely is on the other side, when we are not in earthly form.

The cool thing about CWO moments is that one cannot make them happen, nor can one predict when they may happen. They are an amazing gift for being truly present in the moment. They can happen anywhere, anytime. An extraordinary musical performance may inspire a CWO moment, as may a connection with nature, as in the following example.

I had completed the spring gardening task of planting tomato and pepper plants. Afterwards, I was sitting on the side of the raised bed where our strawberry plants grow, making notes. I happened to glance over at the strawberry plants and the sight was breath-taking. Strawberry leaves are oval-shaped with toothed edges, and at that moment, there was a perfect drop of dew on every tooth of every leaf on every plant in the 8-foot square bed. It was a perfect array of "diamonds" in the bright sunshine. This natural phenomenon was simply there, created with no effort whatsoever. I happened to notice it, but my noticing it had nothing to do with it—it was there, and astoundingly beautiful, whether I had seen it or not. It was CWO moment.

Another time I have experienced this bliss is in watching a spider spin a web. The spider is immersed in very busy and focused activity, but the process is not rushed in any way. It is a gift to take the time to watch this amazing feat. It is mesmerizing, meditative, an opportunity to escape that flurry of thoughts whirling around in the brain. It may even give you a new appreciation for spiders.

I am convinced that we are constantly immersed in these moments of beauty, awe and wonder, but we often don't notice because we are too busy planning the future or fussing over the past. Slow down, breathe, listen and observe.

"If you make listening and observation your occupation you will gain much more than you can by talk." Robert Baden-Powell

To Ponder: Be still and observe. Do this often. What am I beginning to see that I hadn't noticed before? Note CWO moments here.

Ponderings

Curiosity (O)

There are many million-dollar industries in existence today telling us that there is something wrong with us that needs to be fixed. These include personal growth, cosmetic surgery, weight loss and fitness, higher education and fashion, for starters.

I would like to offer a different approach to these options. Instead of using them as a means to fix a defect, let's view them as some of the infinite possibilities we get to experience and learn from and enjoy. I'm suggesting a sense of curiosity rather than a need for fixing. In truth, our height, weight, looks, physical condition, emotions and mental state don't matter except in the way we let them influence how we live our lives.

The feeling of a need to fix is burdensome. Curiosity, however, implies a sense of adventure and wonder. Amazing things can happen when we let curiosity lead us in baby steps. As I look back over my life, I see that my curiosity and a willingness to learn have been huge beneficial components in my life. My first book came into being because I wanted to see if I could get myself to wake up early and write every day. Curiosity has taken me on fabulous travels around the world. It has led me to meet many wonderful people, and even to completely change careers. None of those things would have happened if I was trying to fix myself.

One thing that tends to kill curiosity is the fear of admitting you don't know something. Admitting you don't know is a strength, not a weakness. It's the starting point of adventure. Besides, nowadays there is so much out there to know, nobody could possibly know it all. We are all beginners, always. With Google, curiosity gets easier all the time.

"We keep moving forward, opening new doors, and doing new things, because we're curious and curiosity keeps leading us down new paths." Walt Disney

To Ponder: What do I wonder about? How might I use simple curiosity to learn more and ease into a desired change? To what places might my curiosity lead me? Am I willing to explore?

Ponderings

If I Knew Then What I Know Now (A)

This is somewhat of a touchy topic, as it could easily digress into regrets about life. So for the record, I love my life, and thus would not change anything because I am grateful for all the people, places and events which have brought me to where I am today.

That said, here I go. If I knew then what I know now…

- I would have been even more adventuresome. I was fortunate that my mother loved to travel. She planted the "travel bug" in me. Though I have visited many places, there is still a huge amount of the world left for me to see.
- I would have forgiven sooner and more often, and not taken so many things so personally.
- I would have been more loving toward my body.
- I would not have been so scared of people.
- I would have been considerably more appreciative of my parents.
- I would have bought more real estate, most likely some sort of vacation home on a body of water.
- I would have played more often with my sons.
- I would have done a lot more singing.
- I would have had more dogs as pets.
- I would have started doing yoga much sooner.
- I would have spent more time on a warm, sunny beach.

The cool thing about all these things is that if I choose, I can do any of them now. That's the whole point of this topic – to get us thinking about what we would do differently if we could, then to realize we can, starting right now.

"There are 30,000 days in your life. When I was 24, I realized I'm almost 9,000 days down. There are no warm-ups, no practice rounds, no reset buttons. Your biggest risk isn't failing, it's getting too comfortable. Every day, we're writing a few more words of a story. I wanted my story to be an adventure and that's made all the difference." Drew Houston

To Ponder: Below is my list. How can I begin to make these things a reality now?

If I knew then what I know now, I would...

Ponderings

Life by Bubba (H)

A friend of our family, Amanda, lived for a time in Greece. There she rescued a small dog, named him Bubba, and brought him back to the U.S. with her.

I am not currently a pet owner, though I enjoy animals very much. I especially enjoy observing animals because they are extraordinary teachers of how to live spontaneously. This brings us to Bubba. He is about 15 inches tall and looks like a miniature golden retriever. Amanda did an exceptional job of training him, and he is a very pleasant and well-behaved pup.

Our whole family loves Bubba. He has an awesome ability to wriggle his way into your heart. What's so special about Bubba?

Bubba is a mixed-breed of many varieties. He was living in the streets of a Greek city with his mamma, whose death prompted Amanda's rescue. He does not, however, carry around baggage related to his lowly beginnings as a "street urchin" pup.

Bubba is very content in his "dogness." (The first time I typed that, it came out "godness" – no coincidence there.) He simply seems to love being what he is.

Bubba is always ready for adventure. The adventure of the moment is often a cat or a squirrel, and every such creature is worthy of Bubba's full attention. My husband and sons took Bubba on a hiking trip to Colorado. Concerns for his stamina were completely unnecessary. Bubba led the way on daily hikes of several miles, exploring, investigating and experiencing every bit of the adventure.

If he is tired, he naps. If he needs to go out, he lets someone know. He drinks when he is thirsty. He eats when he is hungry. If he feels like playing, he finds a toy. If he needs loving, he hangs around a human friend. He is always ready for a W-A-L-K, and gets newly excited over every single one. He doesn't worry and fret over what may happen in the future. He knows, even takes for granted, that he is loved and cared for, and he is loyal and adoring in return. He has no qualms about leaving his mark wherever he has been (if you get my drift…). It's not complicated. He lives spontaneously in the moment.

Bubba even taught me something about stereotypes. One time when I was walking with him, we approached a fire hydrant and I thought, "Every dog's dream." Bubba completely ignored it.

I encourage you to live like your pet – they are wise creatures. I expect that is why we get so attached to pets – they draw us back to our inner essence, living and loving in the now.

"Until one has loved an animal, a part of one's soul remains unawakened." Anatole France

To Ponder: What do I love and learn from my interactions with animals? How can I bring more of an animal's joy into my life?

<u>Ponderings</u>

Nothing's Impossible (O)

I am a multi-decade Cubs fan, and have been sadly but faithfully mired in "maybe next year." The Cubs last World Series win was in 1908. I set one of my life's goals to be living long enough to see the Cubs win the World Series again. As I write this, it's after a long, late night seeing that very thing happen. 2016 World Champs!

Everything seemed against the Cubs. They were down three games to one in the Series. They came back. The Cubs' closer maddeningly blew the save in the last game, but ended up getting the win with his team "picking him up" at the plate. There was a 17-minute rain delay after the 9th inning which served as time for an empowering motivational speech by one Cubs player to the rest of the team.

The point of all this: things happen that we can't predict if we simply stay true to our course, holding our goal in mind, keep stepping up to the plate, believing. I've had many instances in my life of the exact resource—person, information, opportunity—showing up when I needed it, as if by magic. It's not magic. It is truly the natural flow of things, the way life is supposed to be. There is great power in allowing ourselves to believe and to be supported by the Universe.

"Nothing is impossible, the word itself says 'I'm possible'!" Audrey Hepburn

To Ponder: What seems impossible to me? How can I take one more step to make the "impossible" happen?

Ponderings

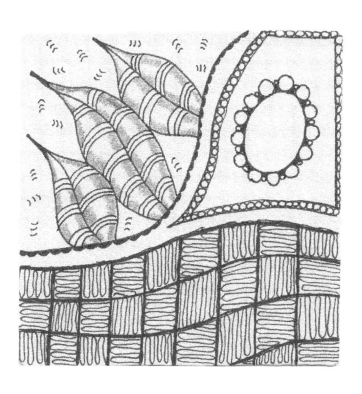

Your God, My God (W/O)

Let's tackle the word "God." It's a human-created three-letter word to represent something that can't be described in words. Therefore, you can call that thing whatever you want… Spirit, Universe, Higher Power, Allah, Buddha, Matilda, Fairy Godmother, Ralph. In my case, Its nickname is "Q." It is the everywhere-present, enlivening energy of all of creation, and It is intelligent.

If you choose, you can have a personal relationship with this life energy. One of the many blessings of a 12-step program is the opportunity to define this presence in any way that makes sense to us. So many folks, including me, grew up with a vengeful, score-keeping, big-meanie god who focused on our sins. It's tough to have a personal relationship with that. I looked at what I needed my god to be for me, and initially, I just needed a big, warm, loving blanket to hold me and assure me that I'm OK. "Q" has evolved over time to be a constant companion with whom I jabber, ask for help, thank, laugh and wonder.

Your god is yours. I hereby give you the freedom to choose a supporting presence in your life that "fills the bill" for you, giving you exactly what you need when you need it. Whatever you imagine is best for you is best for you. There is no judgment involved here, by me or by the presence you create for yourself. Your idea of a higher power can and likely will change over time as you develop a friendship with it. The life energy of the universe is big enough, powerful enough and intelligent enough to be whatever you ask it to be. There's nothing to lose, and so much to be gained, by having a personal relationship with your god.

"My God, my higher power, it's mine and mine alone. I create my connection, and I decide what my connection is going to be." Will Smith

To Ponder: If I could have any higher power of my choosing, what would it be and do in my life? How can I interact with that higher power to strengthen the relationship?

Ponderings

Perfectionism (H)

Perfectionism, I know this well. It's an extremely common "character defect" in an addict, which I am. It has nothing to do with our inherent wholeness as spiritual beings. It is also unrelated to doing our best. Perfectionism is abuse of self first, and others, pure and simple.

All efforts at making something perfect, no matter how well intentioned, come from a place of "not enough." It's a continual striving for an ideal that does not exist in the physical realm, because "perfect" in the physical realm is completely subjective and based on individual judgment. Label something as "perfect," and within seconds a critic will explain why it is not so.

We are killing our children, literally, with demands overt or covert that they be perfect. Why else do they end their own lives other than they feel they don't measure up to the way they "should" be?

Here are some ways that perfectionism may be showing up in your life:

- Not allowing folks into your home because it's not clean enough
- Not trying that new interesting thing because you may not do it perfectly
- Not creating the work of your heart because someone else may find fault with it
- Not liking what you do create because you find fault with it
- Not going to the grocery store in sweats without makeup because someone you know may see you
- Awkwardness in social situations fearing others may not like you
- Thinking that if you could just fix this one thing in yourself or someone else, life would be perfect
- Expecting others to perform in a certain way so as not to embarrass you or to "add feathers to your cap."
- Comparing yourself to others (your insides to their outsides)
- Striving to "keep up with the Joneses"
- Experiencing feelings of shame
- Reluctance to ask for help
- Continually hearing "should" and "shouldn't" in your self-talk

"Perfectionism is a self destructive and addictive belief system that fuels this primary thought: If I look perfect, and do everything perfectly, I can avoid or minimize the painful feelings of shame, judgment, and blame." Brene Brown

To Ponder: In what ways do I see perfectionism infiltrating my life? What am I trying to hide behind that perfectionism?

Ponderings

Judgment (W)

Something within us knows our wholeness. That something was there at birth. Consider a newborn—she does not consider herself fat or short or helpless, she simply does what comes naturally in this new body her spirit has entered. Interaction with a newborn most likely inspired the thought that he or she is "perfect." That's not bias, it's the truth. And it remains the truth throughout our lives.

However, enter family relationships, cultural norms, religious dogma, and education systems, and that spiritual perfection gets buried in the deepest recesses of our soul. Messages of "not enough" become louder and louder. How can one possibly feel complete when the societal norm says that if you feel good about who you are, you are conceited and selfish?

I think there's within us at a very deep level a wondering of how we became so flawed when we were so whole to begin with. There's a yearning to let our true self be what we show to the world, mask-free, pretense-free.

We live in a world that is rampant with judgment. It's everywhere, about everything. Or so it seems. The only reason we are seeing and feeling this judgment surrounding us is because we are judging ourselves and projecting it onto our world. If we stop judging ourselves, the world becomes a much less judgmental place.

"Doubt yourself and you doubt everything you see. Judge yourself and you see judges everywhere. But if you listen to the sound of your own voice, you can rise above doubt and judgment. And you can see forever." Nancy Lopez

To Ponder: What judgments do I place upon myself? How does that self-judgment feel? How does it feel to appreciate myself? How can I expand that self-appreciation?

Ponderings

The Great Waterslide Debate

Here's the dialogue between me and my Inner Roommate while swimming laps at the YMCA:

Me: It would be fun to go down the big waterslide. It's been a long time since I've done that.

IR: Aren't you a little old for that?

Me: I'm never too old to have fun.

IR: You're too fat.

Me: It's plenty sturdy, and stop it! I'm not too fat.

IR: People will think you are silly.

Me: Oh, please, I have evolved way past that.

IR: Don't bug the lifeguard. He doesn't want to turn it on just for you.

Me: The lifeguard is friendly. He'd turn it on.

IR: (Getting nervous) You might get hurt!

Me: OK, next time.

Over and over this dialogue went through my head, three times a week while I was swimming in the lap pool.

Then, yesterday, as good intentions and synchronicity would have it, the waterslide was on as I finished swimming. The lifeguard had turned it on for a woman in the rec pool to work out in the strong current at the bottom of the slide. My moment had come! I quickly climbed out of the lap pool, and went to the lifeguard and asked to go down the slide. That extremely stoic young man got the tiniest of grins on his face, and walked over and unchained the stairs leading to the top. Up I went. My Inner Roommate went nuts… "What ARE you doing?!?! Are you CRAZY?!?!?"

I went down the slide. It was a fast ride, maybe 10 seconds. It was a blast. I shut up my Inner Roommate, at least for a while. I probably set a record for that lifeguard for the oldest person to go down the slide on his watch. There were no injuries, and the "thrill of victory" made my day.

Non-Harming (H)

Yoga is an eight-limb system designed thousands of years ago to promote complete union with the universal life force. It is much more than the postures performed in a typical yoga class. Chances are good that even if you don't do those postures, you are practicing yoga. The system is designed to support us in living a healthy, connected, peaceful, and joyful life.

The yama limb of yoga offers restraints, or things not to do, to live successfully. One of those is to avoid violence or harming. The Sanskrit term is *ahimsa*. OK, fine, you say, I'm not into beating up someone or shooting anything. That's good, but it only hits the surface of this restraint. It applies not only to our actions, but to our thoughts and speech as well.

There are many ways, often unconscious, that we routinely bring harm into our lives: gossiping, comparing ourselves to others, criticizing others, negative self-talk, bullying, controlling others, poor self-care, addictive behavior, an "us vs. them" mentality, judgmentalism, worrying, road rage, cursing, agreeing to something we really don't want to do. It's fairly clear from this partial list that if it doesn't feel good, it's a form of violence or harming, either to ourselves or others.

"At the center of non-violence stands the principle of love." Martin Luther King, Jr.

To Ponder: Pay attention to those situations when I don't feel quite right. Is there harming involved? What am I discovering about myself and my behavior?

<u>Ponderings</u>

Words Matter (H)

Joy fills every cell in my body.
Every cell is alive with love.
I relax into the healing process.
I allow Spirit to do what it does.

These are the lyrics to "The Healing Song," recorded by Karen Drucker.

Whether we choose to believe it or not, research is showing more and more that our bodies respond to the words and thoughts we direct at them. (For more information on this, read "The Biology of Belief" by Bruce Lipton.) While you may think it's silly or "woowoo" to talk positively to your body, why not do it? No one is listening, and it's certain to have a better outcome than critical, negative body-talk.

I have seen first-hand in both myself and many yoga students the power of body-talk. Many students come to yoga with something they'd like to fix about their bodies, i.e., there's something wrong with them. This is a nearly universal mentality, unfortunately. There's a strong initial focus internally on what they can't do, rather than what they can do. I work with them in every class on transforming their minds to recognize the magnificent, intelligent, powerful, adaptive body they live in, and to focus on what it <u>can</u> do.

You don't need to practice yoga, however, to have a good body image. Start by ignoring the media and the ridiculous portrayal of a "perfect body." It doesn't exist. A healthy body is the ideal. I started the improvement of my body image and body-talk with selecting one thing about my body that I am grateful for, and that was my female parts that enabled me to birth two healthy children. From there my appreciation has continued to grow, and I am extremely comfortable in my own skin. I am also very healthy. I express kindness toward my body throughout the day in various ways. I love The Healing Song quoted above—it's a catchy tune that enables me to reinforce the wholeness and magnificent mystery of my body.

Most folks' body-talk is completely unconscious. The negative "tapes" have been running for so long, they don't even notice them. Start with simply observing what you say to your body. It will be an eye-opener.

"The future is to heal back to the mind again. Recognizing that the mind is all powerful - it controls every cell to every degree of its genetic expression." Bruce Lipton

To Ponder: What is my body-talk like? Can I find one thing about my body to appreciate? Here is a positive statement about my body…

Ponderings

Practice (A)

One thing I am especially grateful for that has come from doing yoga is the concept of practice. We hear the word all the time, we get the idea, but few of us actually practice "practice." Yes, athletes and musicians who strive to better their skills are well-versed in practicing. Consistent, repetitive, daily actions are the backbones of practice.

My focus here, however, is that simply living is a practice. We are born mostly helpless, and through practice, we learn to walk, eat solid food, use a toilet, read, etc. We continue doing those things on a daily basis, and some days are better than others as far as these practices go. For instance, it doesn't matter our age, occasionally we still fall down.

Learning to be in relationships is a practice. Nobody is exempt from speaking amiss to a family member or friend and then having to make amends. Relationships continually require compromise, communication, and caring. We learn these things by practicing.

Self-care is another skill that develops via practice. What we eat and drink, how we choose to spend our time, and how we value ourselves change over time as we learn what works for us and what doesn't support us.

Our societal obsession with perfectionism is the antithesis of practice. We are afraid of not doing something perfectly from the get-go, and so we don't even try. How many gifts have never been materialized because the giver was not willing to learn, develop, and practice enough to create the gift?

"It is a full time job being honest one moment at a time, remembering to love, to honor, to respect. It is a practice, a discipline, worthy of every moment." Jasmine Guy

To Ponder: What do I consistently practice in my life? What new skill would I like to learn by practicing?

Ponderings

Choices (W)

Feeling lousy about ourselves is every bit a choice, just as being happy and content is a choice. Though we like to blame our feelings on others, no one outside of us has control over how we feel.

Unfortunately, we think that it is easier to stick with our habitual self-image than it is to select a more pleasing view of ourselves.

We may think that we have a fairly good level of self-esteem, but consider the following list of behaviors as indicators of personal dissatisfaction:

- Blaming others for feelings or experiences
- Guilt and/or shame
- Perfectionism
- People-pleasing
- Working at a dissatisfying or even miserable job
- Putting off dreams and goals to "someday"
- Addictive behaviors—drinking, overeating, gambling, smoking, etc.
- Negativity toward the physical body
- Frequent or chronic illness
- Procrastination
- Unwillingness to complete a project or fulfill a commitment
- Being fearful
- Living based on the words "should" and "shouldn't"
- Being concerned about what others think
- Refusal to forgive
- Habitual tardiness

Freedom of choice is the fundamental operating principle of life on this planet. I believe that experiencing such freedom is why we choose to come here in the first place. We always have a choice. Always! When I assigned my sons a "no-negotiations" chore, I told them they still had the choice to adopt a good attitude or a bad attitude about it. Feeling you have no choice is very disempowering, and definitely not supportive of self-esteem. The ultimate point of choice for us humans is our thoughts, and we choose those in every moment.

"Freedom of choice is more to be treasured than any possession earth can give." David O. McKay

To Ponder: Do I see myself in any of the behaviors listed above? In what situation(s) do I feel I have no choice? What are my choices?

Ponderings

Contentment (H)

The *niyama* limb of the eight-limb system of yoga offers practices that enhance life. One of those is *santosha*, which translates to contentment. Contentment is a state that one can cultivate and expand with practice.

Let's look first at what contentment is not. It's not resignation, as in, "I don't like this, but I'll live with it." Contentment is not achieved by the acquisition of material things, praise, acclaim or rewards. It is also not a continuous state, nor should we burden ourselves by expecting it to be. Human beings are simply not perfect at the practice of contentment.

Contentment is a feeling, and if you pay attention to your body (also a life-long practice), you can detect that feeling somewhere within your body. Each person is different in where they feel emotions, but our bodies do reflect these feelings. For me, contentment is centered around my heart.

Not feeling contentment is not necessarily a bad thing. Often it is discontent with a current situation that encourages us to make beneficial changes. Feelings of dissatisfaction are the warning sign that we have drifted from our contentment practice. We humans can muddle around for very long periods of time, decades even, in those feelings of discontent until the discomfort simply becomes unbearable. Dreams discarded, but not forgotten, are often a relentless source of discontent.

Here are some ways that contentment shows up in my life:

- I have an excellent, intimate relationship with a higher power.
- I enjoy the work I do, and it's a good use and expression of my talents.
- I love my home and family and the community in which I live.
- I enjoy, even need, lots of time to myself.
- All my basic needs are abundantly met, and I feel secure.
- I love many folks, and I am bountifully loved in return.
- I devote considerable time and effort to maintaining both my physical and spiritual well-being.
- I generally follow my intuition.
- Flexibility of my schedule is important to me, and I've been able to arrange my working life to support that priority.
- I am able to use my talents in service to others.
- I am able regularly to do those things I especially enjoy, such as traveling and golfing.

"Contentment is the only real wealth." Alfred Nobel

To Ponder: What does contentment mean to me? What is my contentment level? Is there a nagging feeling of discontent within me? What is its message?

Ponderings

Never Waste a Good Trigger (O/A)

This is a quote from Ana Forrest, the wonderful woman and spiritual mentor who taught me to be a yoga teacher. What is a trigger?

We have all had our buttons pushed. There's that person who just keeps pushing it, despite our best efforts. That recurring work situation makes us crazy. A particular place or event gives us the creeps. All of these things that create unsettled feelings in us are triggers.

What does this title quote mean? It suggests that we use these people, places, events, and relationships to examine what's going on within ourselves that causes us to set out our buttons to be pushed. Any time we are triggered, that person or situation is mirroring to us something in ourselves that we don't like. Things we don't like in ourselves tend to get lodged in our bodies and spirits, and they create discomfort of a mental, emotional, and physical nature. These discomforts are messengers, meant for us to learn from them, and let them go. So triggers actually are a spiritual cleansing device.

Here's an example. Being raised by a card-carrying perfectionist, I am a natural born rule-follower. (That's another topic in this book.) Thus, when I see someone breaking a "rule," such as driving incorrectly or checking out with too many items in the express aisle, it triggers a "rule-breaker" response in me. Really? Are these items important enough to disturb my inner peace? What I realized is that these are bumping my perfectionist button. People will be people. Many are not rule-followers. Neither they nor I need to be perfect. I can observe, move on, and stay peaceful, smiling at our erratic human behaviors.

"Every burden bears a gift, every challenge brings a treasure, and every setback hides a blessing." Mike Dooley

To Ponder: What people, places and situations push my buttons? What can I learn about myself from each of these triggers?

Ponderings

"Cover Me Up!"

When our younger son, Eliot, was about four years old, he developed a nightly habit of waking up in the middle of the night having kicked off his blankets. Upon this discovery, he'd start yelling, "Cover me up!" Either my husband or I, in our half-asleep stupor, would oblige, in order to shut him up and get back to sleep as soon as possible.

Eventually, when we were both wide awake, my husband and I came to the obvious realization that Eliot was perfectly capable of covering himself. It was time to stop acquiescing to his demands. One evening before bed, we let Eliot know clearly that we were not going to get up and cover him, that he is a big boy and very much able to do that himself.

Eliot tested us, as children will blissfully do. The yelling began, "Cover me up!" Our bedroom door, directly across the hall from Eliot's room, was closed and locked, so that he could not get in to wake us. Of course, we were awake due to the yelling. Once Eliot realized that we were, in fact, not going to cover him up, his fury knew no bounds. He threw everything he could lift in his room at our bedroom door, screaming such things as "I hate you!" with every hurl. My husband and I stuck to our commitment, and I'll confess, we were quite amused as we listened to the tantrum on the other side of our bedroom door.

When he exhausted his supply of projectiles, Eliot stopped, said, "I go back to bed now," covered himself up, and went back to sleep. That was the last night we heard, "Cover me up!"

Fast forward to Eliot's teen years. Every so often over the next 10 years, he would let us know that he was still angry with us about that incident. He was convinced we were mean, and bad parents, to boot. Granted, those beliefs are common among all teenagers, but this incident was an especially raw wound for him. I've listened patiently, letting him know he is heard, while silently saying to myself, "There are some things you'll never understand until you are a parent yourself."

Fast forward again. Eliot, in his later 20s, is in a lovely relationship with a woman who has a four-year-old daughter. On a recent visit, he and I were talking, and he said to me, "Mom, I finally get the 'cover me up!' thing." Holy cow, what joy, for him, for me and my husband, for empowering our children to be resourceful and independent! Parenting ain't easy, but it sure is fun and enlightening.

Rent-Free Living (A)

"You're letting him live in your head rent-free." Arlen Miller

I was once mired in an ongoing work situation caused by the actions of one particular person and the fallout that resulted. Many folks were dragged into and through the slop. It was all-consuming for months. Eventually I was feeling completely drained by it, and I spoke to my older brother, Arlie, about it. That's when he spoke the above quote to me. Whoa! What a wake-up call!

As I am writing this, we have just survived in the U.S. the nastiest presidential campaign and election in my six-decade lifetime. Regardless of whether your pick won or lost, whether you are delighted or depressed, you have the choice of letting the President live in your head rent-free. Do you want to do that?

The only thing of significance that we really have control over is our thoughts. This is huge, because it is our thoughts that shape our experience. So it doesn't matter who is President—what matters is what we think about that person. If we believe that leader will take us down a path of destruction, that's all we'll see. If we believe we can rise above and live a life of wholeness and well-being on every level, that's what we'll continue to experience. Again, who is the President (or governor or pope or boss or relative) does not matter.

"Live light. Offload internal and external baggage for peace within and peace without."
Laurie Buchanan

To Ponder: Who/what am I letting live in my head rent-free? Is it time for some house-cleaning and maybe even a few evictions?

Ponderings

Bacon & Butter (H)

My husband and I recently sat down to enjoy another of his wonderful, home-cooked meals, and it resulted in the profound statement, "Bacon and butter make everything better."

We all have our "secret" indulgences which we really love, but don't want to admit it. It may be chocolate, mac 'n' cheese, carrot cake, marshmallow cream, or any of a zillion other supposedly naughty foods.

A friend and I recently went on an adventure to Scotland and Ireland. I was delighted to find mac 'n' cheese on nearly every pub menu. Truly the Scots and Irish know how to eat well. And yes, I thoroughly enjoyed their mac 'n' cheese, completely guilt-free.

Why hide? Why not indulge on occasion? This is just one more instance in life where we drag in guilt and invite it to dine with us. I'm no stranger to meal-time strife. My childhood was a continual volley of "Have some more!" and "You'd be really cute if you'd lose weight." Needless to say, learning to enjoy food and eat guilt-free has been a long-term process.

I'm not suggesting carrot cake at every meal, but rather creating a joyous environment around food preparation and eating, really enjoying every bite, guilt-free, no matter what it is. It's a huge part of life's pleasure to have so many wonderful foods available to us.

"Some days you eat salads and go to the gym, other days you eat cupcakes and refuse to put on pants. It's called balance." Anonymous

To Ponder: What's my "secret" food indulgence? Why do I hide it? How does guilt play into this?

Ponderings

Personal Management Team (W/O)

One can think of God, or the Universe, or the One Supreme Intelligence as a personal management team (PMT) working tirelessly on one's behalf. For instance, my management team is currently busy with supporting my writing efforts. At every moment, I am making choices. That's what living spontaneously is—making choices at each instance what to do, be or have in that moment. It's a harrowing life for a PMT, but I know that my team is up to it.

Ancient spiritual wisdom and modern quantum physics tell us that there really are no such things as time and space, that we have created those things in order to take form and experience life in this earthly realm. With no such thing as time and space, anything I ask for with my thoughts is instantly created or chosen from infinite possibilities. So the answer to what is commonly referred to as prayer is already there, already existing without the constraints of time and space. Taking delivery is the issue. We have conditioned ourselves to have to wait for the answer to prayer. Having to wait is the root of what seems to be unanswered prayer. We may spiritually forget that we asked, or we are "out to lunch" when the delivery arrives, or we change our minds and refuse delivery.

While in earthly form, we have accepted the judgments of "big" and "little" and "difficult" and "easy" relative to possibilities. For instance, curing cancer is difficult while healing a cut finger is easy. A checking account of $10 million is big and one of $247 is little. There are no such judgments within Spirit. Those are all simply choices among the infinite possibilities available at any given moment. Every heart's desire is the same to your PMT.

Use of a PMT may involve a rather drastic change of mindset that is often difficult for a person. That would be asking for help. We have to ask. We've been so conditioned in our culture that to ask for help is bothersome or a sign of weakness. It's just the opposite, truly a sign of humble strength to know our limitations and seek support when needed.

"Teamwork makes the dream work." Anonymous

To Ponder: What would I like my PMT to do for me? Ask!

Ponderings

Pay Attention (A)

Lots of unfortunate things happen when we aren't paying attention, such as falls, miscommunication, getting lost, and car accidents. There are several ways in which we don't pay attention.

One distraction is hanging out in the past, reviewing our prior miscues, or what didn't get done, or what we ought to have said. We can expend a lot of energy feeling bad about the past. We can even expend a lot of energy reliving good times from the past and wishing those times could be "now" again.

We can get carried away into the future, where we worry about what might happen (but usually doesn't). How will we act? What will others do in response? Will I succeed? What if I fail? What if? What if? It wears me out just writing about it.

Up until recently, the ability to multi-task has been seen as an asset. How could it not be? Being able to do two or three things at the same time has to be awesome. Actually, it is not, because the multi-tasker, it turns out, isn't really paying attention to any of the several tasks. It is distracted, inefficient work.

The ability to stay within the present moment is the key to paying attention. The simplest way to be present is to focus on breathing. Another technique I use is to remind myself that I am not in a hurry, slow down. (Even if I am in a hurry, it is not so urgent that I want to cause an accident.) Our thinking tends to get on autopilot, so if we can reign that in and break the habitual thinking, it makes it easier to pay attention to what's happening now. If you're with others, really looking at them and listening carefully helps to stay present-focused. Last but not least, the simple reminder "pay attention!" works wonders.

"Tell me to what you pay attention and I will tell you who you are." Jose Ortega y Gasset

To Ponder: When do I notice myself not paying attention? How might I change those situations to be more attentive?

Ponderings

Resiliency (W)

We humans are born helpless, and spend a lifetime at the practice of learning to take care of ourselves. The first thing we discover that works well is crying, the louder the better. That gets attention and usually gets us back to a comfy state. Eventually we learn to crawl, which gets us to that interesting shiny object over there. Wow, we can move. Then we notice that those humans around us are up there and moving on their feet, maybe we can, too. We want to go fast like them.

There is a natural organic process at work here. We develop strength (physical, emotional, spiritual) through adversity. Tough times cause us to consider a couple of questions. What are my choices in this situation? What tools have I used in the past to help me overcome an adverse situation such as this?

As a parent and life coach, I have encountered numerous instances where parents feel their parenting success depends upon keeping anything bad from happening to their children, ever. This truly does not serve the youngsters in the long run, as they do not develop the resiliency to handle the ups and downs that will surely come in their lives. As a simple example, each of our sons fell down our carpeted stairs once, just a few stairs, tough to watch. But that experience taught them, instantly, that there must be better ways to get down the stairs, and it would be a good thing to figure that out, and quickly.

The 12-step programs are all about resiliency for addicts, giving them an organized path for improving their choices and a set of tools that have worked to help other addicts recover.

Emiliya Zhivotovskaya (emiliya.com) is a psychologist who focuses on post-traumatic growth, our ability to use trauma as a catalyst for positive change, thriving, and expanding our resilience. Positive psychology and resiliency are hot topics of study nowadays, should you care to explore.

"Obstacles, of course, are developmentally necessary; they teach us strategy, patience, critical thinking, resilience and resourcefulness." Naomi Wolf

To Ponder: What traumas have I experienced? How have they strengthened me? What tools do I have to support me through future challenges? How can I support resiliency in those I love?

Ponderings

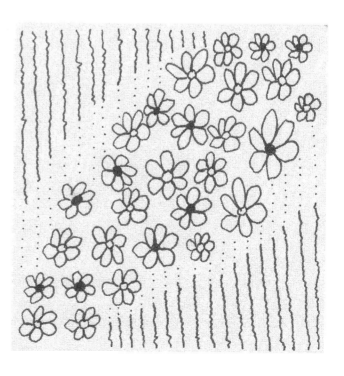

Ken, My Greatest Teacher

I was born when my brothers were in their mid-teens. Being a surprise to everyone except Mom, I was the complete joy and delight of the family and extended family, except for one person, my brother Ken. Squeezed between a smart, super-athletic, bound-for-West-Point older brother and the princess, he became a nasty, lost soul. Alas, the nastiness was taken out on me, life-long. As life and luck would have it, he turned out to be my life's greatest teacher.

I can't imagine having had a baby when my sons were in their mid-teens. It would have been total chaos. I'm sure that was the case when I arrived. Ken, therefore, had an easy target, a helpless child, on which to take out his angst. Throughout my lifetime, he always used teasing as a cover-up for his intense despising of me. There was plenty of verbal abuse.

Two instances of physical abuse are worth noting. As a young child he used to set me on top of the refrigerator and leave me there, where I was too terrified to try to climb down. One time he, Mom and I were in the kitchen. I was probably in the 3-years-old range. Ken was seated, holding me standing between his legs, teasing me, wouldn't let me go. So I leaned in and bit him on his fat stomach, drawing blood. He didn't do that to me again.

I share these instances to point out the behavior of teasing. It is not harmless. For the teaser, it is a blatant but unconscious display of "I feel bad about myself, so I want to make you feel even worse than I do." For the person being teased, it puts you continually in a defensive stance. Sometimes I fought back, a useless effort that only escalated the teasing, or I tolerated it, a self-defeating place of "You're right, I'm not good enough." It was vicious psychological warfare on Ken's part.

One mighty lesson I learned from my upbringing around Ken is that a bad example can be a good thing. At least one learns how <u>not</u> to behave. While Ken worked hard at his job and supported his family, the rest of the time he laid on the couch and demanded that Mary Ellen, his wife, wait on him. He left the raising of their four children to her. Fortunately there was extended-family help, including me, for Mary Ellen. The best thing Ken ever did was marry Mary Ellen, as she was the epitome of love as much as he was the epitome of nastiness.

Ken's influence on my life ultimately led me to learn the healing power of forgiveness. It's a healing and cleansing process for the person doing the forgiving. It has been a saving grace for me that I was finally able to let go of my dislike and accept him as the hurting, lost soul that he was. I do appreciate all that I've learned from being in a family relationship with him.

Ken's constant teasing and verbal abuse, my being the youngest child and only girl, and multiple addictions in my family of origin, ultimately taught me that I had to stand up for myself, no one else would. Messages of "not good enough" were strong in my family. Ken was an expert at blaming others for his miseries. Little wonder I came out of there with an addictive personality. It did, however, drive me to recovery and taking responsibility for my life. I have learned to stand up for myself and release the "not good enough" chatter in my head.

It has not been a pretty journey. There have been lots of tears of rage. The forgiveness happened on my end, but not his. Once I left Pennsylvania, we had little contact except at the occasional family get-togethers. Neither one of us was the sort of person the other one would have wanted to hang around. Our only connection was having the same set of parents. We did not speak the last five years of his life. When he was dying of cancer, he ordered his children not to notify me. No surprise there.

He served me well as a powerful teacher. I believe it was an act of love that he agreed to before we ever arrived here. This passage from "Radical Forgiveness" by Colin Tipping describes us perfectly:

> **"Ironically, the people who seem to upset us the most are those who, at the soul level, love and support us the most. Almost always, and often at great expense to themselves in terms of their own discomfort, these individuals try to teach us something about ourselves and to encourage us to move towards healing. Remember, this is not a personality-to-personality exchange. In fact, more than likely, the personalities of these individuals clash terribly. Instead, the souls of each player set up the scenario in the hope that the person will eventually see their issue and heal."**

Job well done, brother! Thank you!

Please Don't (A)

I have a friend who was once charged with the task of finding helpers for Vacation Bible School, and I was on her call list. Though she knew my answer, she did her duty and contacted me and asked. I said, "You know I don't like kids! No!" We had a good laugh.

I could have certainly guilted myself into helping, but I would have hated every second. I'm not a kid person. I can take them in small doses, but I feel totally uncomfortable amongst a group of little ones. Had I said "yes" to helping, I would have brought a lot of negativity to the event, which would have helped no one, especially the children.

I worked at a church office for several years, and churches are a hotbed for people getting guilted into positions they don't really want. A classic example was folks on the finance committee who could not read a financial statement, nor did they care to learn.

We know in our hearts whether something really appeals to us or if we are considering it because we "should." Please don't go for the "should" option. If it doesn't feel right and appealing to you, it is someone else's job. Be bold. Say "no." You'll be doing others a favor. Thank you!

P.S. There is no need whatsoever to justify your refusal. A simple "no" will do.

'If something is not a "hell, YEAH!", then it's a "no!"' James Altucher

To Ponder: Have I ever agreed to do something I really did not want to do? How did that feel? Why did I not say "no"? How can I be more true to my heart's wisdom in the future?

Ponderings

Lighten Up (A)

Oh, my, we do take ourselves so seriously! We are especially fond of trying to fix people and unpleasant circumstances. There really is no need to fix anything. We are here to enjoy ourselves. Think on this a bit—if every single person on the planet is content and easy-going about his or her life, would there be any wars, terrorism, people running amok? No.

We humans have very little in life over which we have any real control, but you'd never guess that from the way folks act. We expend an extraordinary amount of effort trying to keep "our ducks in a row," seemingly very serious business.

The nearly-universal automatic response from parents when asked what they want for their children is "I want them to be happy." How can they be happy if we as parents don't model it for them? Don't work so hard on your to-do list (the important stuff finds a way to get done). Figure out what is fun for you and do more of it. Enjoy the people in your life. Relax your schedule. Reduce your commitments. Breathe and smile.

"I am thankful for laughter, except when milk comes out my nose." Woody Allen

To Ponder: How many times a day do I laugh? Is that enough? How can I bring more laughter and lightness into my day?

Ponderings

Simple Kindness (A)

Kindness is a spiritual practice. It's a way of living, not simply a kind action now and then. There are five simple ways to practice kindness throughout the day:

1. Smile. Smiling feels good, and invites others to respond the same way (though they may not, and that doesn't matter). It creates positive energy even in the briefest of interactions when you are being friendly and open.
2. Say "please." As Abraham-Hicks says, "Nobody came here to be the keeper of you." When you ask for something, be polite. This is an especially important practice to use with those closest to you, your most frequent interactions. Folks are much more willing to be helpful if you say "please."
3. Say "thank you." When you experience kindness, acknowledge it. Appreciate others for the help and service they provide. Everyone blossoms with appreciation.
4. Say "you're welcome." It's a pet peeve of mine to hear "no problem" when I say "thank you." It makes me want to say, "So glad I didn't bother you." It's just as easy to say "you're welcome," so make it a habit.
5. Look at other people with interest. So often we don't really see those with whom we are interacting—either we take them for granted, or we're too mired in our own mental chatter or electronic devices to notice. Be present, pay attention to the person in front of you. Remember to use 1-4 above as appropriate.

"Wherever there is a human being, there is an opportunity for a kindness." Lucius Annaeus Seneca

To Ponder: Reminder to self: practice at least one of these kindness techniques today and notice how it feels. Consider my daily interactions—am I really paying attention to the other person(s)? How can I improve my kindness practice?

<u>Ponderings</u>

Reframing (O)

One glorious fall day I was walking at a local park, enjoying my usual meditative mental musings. I passed a woman walking with a cane, using it as a cane, but it was gnarled like a walking stick. It led me to thinking of the many ways I've learned to reframe common things into a more positive light. Doesn't "walking stick" feel better than "cane"? Walking stick ignites thoughts of adventure, while cane makes one think of barely getting around.

Despite periods of full-time employment, I've spent generally around half my life as a housewife. There's nothing wrong with that label. I've served in that role happily. However, I've come to refer to that role as "domestic goddess." That feels way more fun, and it's especially helpful for accomplishing my least favorite chore of cleaning.

Another favorite reframing is related to crying. I refer to it as soul-rinsing. Folks are often embarrassed by their crying, or resistant to it, even though it's a very important physical capability. Soul-rinsing is really more accurate, as the act of crying is usually a spiritually cleansing process.

I also use another reframing instance with my yoga students. Abdominal work is a part of every class, and newer students often find that this causes muscle soreness the day after. Instead of using "soreness," I let them know that they may experience "energy moving in places it was not moving before." That's a good thing, and again, it feels better than "you may be sore."

Here are a few more examples: nosey-curious, stubborn-persistent, daydreamer-creative, indecisive-deliberate.

"If you change the way you look at things, the things you look at change." Wayne Dyer

To Ponder: In what instances in my life can I take a negative term or concept and make it more positive?

Ponderings

Lions & Coyotes, Oh My! (H/A)

Sometimes you just gotta blow off some energy. Every now and then I have my yoga classes hold a pose and do lion roars or coyote howls. For a lion roar, take a huge inhale, open your mouth as wide as you can, stick out your tongue and ROAR like a lion. For a coyote howl, take a giant inhale, tilt your head back and howl like a coyote. The idea is to be as loud as possible, releasing lots of pent-up energy.

Sounds simple, doesn't it? There are deep roots in this learned skill, which relate to one's willingness to be heard and speak up for oneself. Even in the safe environment of a class where one is encouraged to make noise, initial attempts at this practice are usually lame at best. Women, especially, are often afraid to make noise. Some claim they can't do it, but with practice and encouragement, most will eventually get loud.

This is an excellent releasing technique, and a great place to use it is when you are alone in your car. No one will know. I've used it when I'm nervous about the event I'm attending, when I'm stuck in horrid traffic, or when I've just left a situation feeling frustrated or angry. You don't even need to have a reason. Roars and howls are a great way to energize yourself.

"I was the shyest human ever invented, but I had a lion inside me that wouldn't shut up!"
Ingrid Bergman

To Ponder: In a private space, let loose a lion roar or coyote howl. Was it weak or powerful? Can I make it louder? How does it feel to make noise?

Ponderings

A Better Idea (O/A)

We humans tend to fall into habitual patterns, sometimes known as traditions, and repeat them without thinking, no matter how cumbersome or annoying the process may become. Then one day, we awaken enough to come up with a better idea.

Here's an example from my life. I have 11 great-nieces and great-nephews on my Miller side of the family. All of them live hundreds of miles away. At Christmas time, I would contact their parents (five sets) to get ideas for gifts. Then I would go shopping, wrap the gifts, prepare them for shipping, take them to the post office, (usually) wait in line, and pay another chunk of money to send them on their way. Exhausting. And those toys or books or games are no doubt long gone.

The better idea that I came up with is this: when my father passed in 2000, I received a small inheritance, and I used some of that to create a "Great Kids Fund," an investment account for the benefit of those children. I added a small monthly sum to it, and over time, it has grown nicely. Each Christmas, I send the parents a letter reporting the Fund's value and the amount of each child's share. When the niece or nephew graduates from high school, I send them a letter announcing their gift, and the option to take it or let it grow. If they don't take it, by age 23, I transfer the shares to them. It's a free gift—they can do whatever they choose with it, no strings attached. This has turned out to be awesome fun, and no more Christmas shopping exhaustion. Plus it supports the practice of saving and investing, a practice to which I am strongly committed. This better idea is a win-win for all.

"New ideas pass through three periods: 1) It can't be done. 2) It probably can be done, but it's not worth doing. 3) I knew it was a good idea all along!" Arthur C. Clarke

To Ponder: Is there a cumbersome habit or tradition that I really don't enjoy? What would be a better idea? Is there anything holding me back from the change?

Ponderings

Change

Yuck. Most of us don't even like hearing the word. It seems as though we are always under the threat of change, be it something forced on us by circumstances or an internal mandate to live differently.

It's a generally common human trait that we don't choose to change until there is great pain involved. Witness the addict hitting bottom or a terminal diagnosis or a dissolving relationship as examples. On rare occasions, we will change without pain, but if you look over your life, you'll most likely see that the primary motivator for change has been some sort of pain.

Here's a non-pain change story, offered with the realization that this is definitely a "first world problem." As I write this, I'm in my early 60s, and I have <u>never</u> had an artificial Christmas tree. The Miller family business was a sawmill in central Pennsylvania. My dad made a living out of cutting down trees and producing lumber, so it was only natural to use his tree-scoping skills to find the best real tree for Christmas. My husband and I have been going to a local Wichita tree farm, Prairie Pines, for our entire married lives. He has always been our tree-feller. Our sons have only ever known real Christmas trees. I love the smell of a real tree in our house.

This year, we won't be home for Christmas (going to visit the sons), and we are not having any parties or events at our house prior to Christmas. With an absolutely agonized feeling in my gut, I broached the subject to my husband of getting a fake tree in an effort to simplify our Christmas preparations. I nearly choked getting the suggestion out. Lengthy discussion of pros and cons ensued, even accompanied by tears (me, not my husband). This is a monumental C-H-A-N-G-E. It even includes thoughts of my parents rolling in their graves. Please understand that if <u>you</u> use a fake tree, fine, no problem, that's your house and your choice. I don't care. I'm not opposed to fake trees, except in my home.

My husband, Dennis, in his steadfast calm way, suggested that we simply investigate artificial trees. He grew up with artificial trees, so he was quite level-headed in the face of this change. We each went to various stores, plus I had a recommendation from a friend for an especially good brand. I also did online research. We learned that you can spend an insane amount of money for a fake tree, especially if you are a Christmas-light-freak like me and want multi-function, ultra-cool lights.

I ended up getting a helluva deal on the "especially good brand" of tree on ebay, an unlit tree, and ordered separate multi-function, ultra-cool lights from Target. The agonized feeling in my gut over this whole change is still with me. My calm, steadfast husband keeps reminding me that we are just trying it out, we don't have to stay with the fake tree forever if it doesn't "work" for us.

The ebay shipping notification on the tree said it might arrive as late as December 23, so I added to my general angst the worry that we might not have ANY tree until nearly Christmas. I threw up a prayer for shipping help, and it was magically answered. The tree and lights arrived just <u>three</u> days after I purchased them online.

My husband unpacked and assembled the tree, marveling at how the process works and how life-like and "random" the very-full branches are. I went away and sewed during the assembly, as I couldn't stand being in the room. I did peek in and take a photo here and there as the tree "grew."

I finally became comfortable enough to get the tree fully decorated with the multi-function, ultra-cool lights. One item to note—I have antique glass bead strings from my childhood tree that my mom gave me, and I could not bear to put those on a fake tree. That would have caused my mom to actually leave the grave she was rolling in and come and haunt us.

The tree is beautiful. I still have some physical angst about it, but I'm warming up to it. It certainly was much easier to trim than a real tree. And there was no obvious killing involved.

However, there remained the task of breaking the news to the sons of an artificial tree being in the house they grew up in. I expected them to freak beyond imagining, making me freak even further. I thought of doing this—as we are driving away from their house after Christmas, put down the window and yell, "We got a fake tree! Love you!" That would be a chicken maneuver. I could also have one sit on each side of me and show them the assembly photos I took. Again, freakage would ensue. I don't want to spoil our brief Christmas time together over this.

Off we go on the day before Christmas Eve to Fort Collins to be with our sons for the holiday. I think Dennis and I were both secretly hoping no mention would be made of a tree at our house. On Christmas morning we were merrily opening gifts in our one-person-at-a-time-in-specific-order routine, when Eliot said, "Did you guys get a tree this year?" Instantaneously, I started crying and Dennis started laughing. Our sons were shocked. Then Derek said, "Did you go to Prairie Pines?" and I cried harder. I sobbed out, "We got a fake tree!" They were not nearly as upset about the tree as they were about me crying and Dennis laughing so suddenly. They simply wanted the assurance that we were not abandoning a live tree forever, to which we heartily agreed. We all recovered and went on to celebrate an outstanding and blessed Christmas together, and the fake tree didn't matter much at all.

Moral of the story: most change is way bigger in our heads than in actual life.

Postscript: Dennis and I were both ill after Christmas, so we were really glad to not have to deal with a real tree and its un-trimming and disposal.

Love or Fear, Which Is It? (A)

In each moment, we have a choice. That is to live in love or to live in fear. Although we are created from and as love, most of us have been conditioned that the world is a scary place, so it seems much easier to live in fear than love.

On a recent errand, I saw a bumper sticker that indicated the car's occupant was a member of a group I have disliked intensely, because I perceive them as racist. Instantly it occurred to me that in disliking that group, I am being just as racist as they are. Geez. That's not the conscious choice I want to make.

I consider myself to be relatively enlightened (while still having infinite potential along those lines!). Therefore, I <u>know</u> that I have the responsibility to choose love, rather than have the knee-jerk reaction of fear, hatred, us vs. them, I'm right—you're wrong.

What does it matter, if I, just one person, choose love? Every one of us affects the consciousness of humanity. I recognize my responsibility to choose love, so I must do that, for me to live well, but also to expand human consciousness toward peace. Just think how our world would be if we all consciously chose love.

This is a big responsibility, it feels overwhelming. Where do you start? Offer a simple blessing to those that would lead you into fear. It's a win-win practice.

"Being angry makes frightened people feel safer." Bob Luckin

"You either move toward something you love or away from something you fear. The first expands, the second constricts." Tom Crum

To Ponder: Where do I exhibit the choice of fear in my life? What can I do to express love instead?

Ponderings

ADIP (W)

Another Day in Paradise. Many folks use this phrase in a sarcastic sense, but I don't. I use it via initials every day in my journaling. This is paradise, should we choose to see it that way. It's merely a choice. The beloved spiritual teacher, Edwene Gaines, says, "Earth is the party planet, didn't you know?" I personally love to subscribe to and live that sentiment.

One vacation morning I went to a coffee shop in Fort Collins for a morning brew and to sit quietly and read. As I settled my stuff at the counter by the front window, I noticed slips of paper under the plexiglass countertop with sayings written on them. My eyes landed first on this: "We see what we create." Amen and amen! I believe my life keeps getting better and better. ADIP is what I create, and that's what I continue to see... a life that keeps getting better. Another way I often state this is "I lead a charmed life."

Does all this mean my life is perfect, I never get upset, that no one ever crosses me? Hell, no! Those bumps in the road are my opportunities to practice my creating abilities. Am I creating more suffering for myself in unpleasant situations, or am I choosing to bring myself back to paradise? Response times vary, trust me, but I'm learning.

My coffee shop visit had an extra-sweet addition. A long-time Chicagoan saw me through the window in my Cubs gear (going to a Cubs-Rockies game) and came in to talk with me and cheer on the Cubs. We had a lovely, joyous conversation. What a fun human connection!

"Paradise is open to all kind hearts." Pierre Jean de Beranger

To Ponder: What part of my day can I recognize as a bit of paradise? How can I expand paradise in my everyday life?

Ponderings

Everything Has a Lifespan (O)

Oh, my, how with just the right words, at just the right time, when I am at just the right level of awareness, so much becomes clear. And afterwards, there's that DUH! feeling, which to me is an indicator of some concept moving from my head to my heart.

I was participating in a webinar with one of my mentors, Dr. Chris Michaels, and he was speaking of how everything has a lifespan. Here's the quote he offered:

"Spiritual leaders know that everything has a lifespan. An approach or strategy that used to work perfectly in an organization will go through a period where it moves from totally effective to completely ineffective. In the end, everything must change and everything that used to work, stops working. Those who resist this natural phenomenon will become stagnant and immaterial. Those who embrace it will adapt to change by creating new strategies and remain relevant."

Everything, whether in an organization or life in general, has a lifespan. Aside from the obvious human lifespan, friendships may fade, marriages dissolve, cars wear out, fads pass, jobs end. For years I had struggled mightily with the concepts of failure and disappointment. This idea of lifespan ends that struggle. I am completely content with the idea of things naturally and organically passing into other more dynamic things. Oh, yes, it's a DUH!, I realize. But it takes a huge burden off my spirit, and for that I am grateful.

"In the life of the spirit there is no ending that is not a beginning." Henrietta Szold

To Ponder: Where has an ending caused me grief or disappointment or a sense of failure? How can I use this lifespan idea to find comfort?

Ponderings

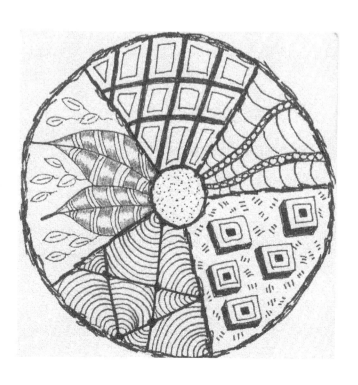

That Moment When You Know, and It Hurts Like Hell

My beloved dad, known by most as Snapper, lived about half of his adult life having periodic mini-strokes. "I'm just having one of my spells," he'd say. At the time we thought they were just bad headaches, and of course, he refused to seek any medical help.

As time progressed and Snapper aged, the "spells" became more frequent, but he recovered fairly well for a man in his 70s. Still he refused medical treatment. Finally, one of the "spells" was severe enough to land him in the hospital, and the doctor easily identified it as a stroke, and brain analysis revealed that this had been an ongoing series of events for quite some time. Again he recovered, and he was still able to live independently.

My dad lived in Pennsylvania and my family lives in Kansas, so my two sons, Derek and Eliot, and I made frequent trips east to see Dad. It was mutual adoration between my sons and Grandpa Snapper. He had even made the huge drive west when Derek was born. Comically enough, it took him three days to drive west, he stayed one day and drove three days home—he did not like being away from home for long.

The boys and I were visiting Dad in the mid-90s, and the four of us, my two brothers, and other assorted family members went out to eat together at a favorite burger bar. Derek, Eliot, and I were sitting directly across the table from my dad. We were having general conversation, enjoying being together, when Dad said to me, " Where are your boys?"

It's amazing how much can happen in an instant. I was shocked, and without thinking said, "Dad, they're right here," and pointed to them. Then this look came over his face. He knew. I knew. It was horrible. The hurt simply can't be described.

His health and mental capacity continued to decline, with ongoing small strokes. He eventually moved to a nursing home, and for the last couple of years didn't know any of the family. He passed on September 24, 2000, the same date on which my mom passed in 1979. I still miss him every day.

Peaceful vs. Right (A)

Would you rather be peaceful or right? I guess the best of all possible worlds would be both, but if you have to choose, which is it?

The 2016 presidential election in the U.S. really brought this question to the forefront for me. It seems that everyone felt the need to be right and no one was peaceful.

I notice that the need to be right narrows the mind and makes one unwilling to consider other viewpoints. The need to be right causes a whole lot of talking and very limited listening. The person who is right is "good" and those who are not right are "bad." The need to be right is a never-ending effort of trying to convince others who "should" be saved from their own ignorance. The need to be right certainly does involve considerable arrogance, and at the same time, insecurity. It's an energy-wasting internal battle.

Then there's the choice to be peaceful. Live and let live. Practice silence. Listen. Learn. Consider. Breathe. Keep an open mind. I'm not even certain that we can absolutely know what is right anyway. Right is such a nebulous concept, like perfect. Each person is entitled to his own opinion, and each one of those will vary because we all have a unique perception of any situation. If you've ever tried to change the mind of someone who knows they are right, you know it's a hopeless waste of time and breath.

Long-term change will not come from those who need to be right. It will come from those who, more than anything, desire peace.

"Other people do not have to change for us to experience peace of mind. I can have peace of mind only when I forgive rather than judge." Gerald Jampolsky

To Ponder: Note a situation in which I feel the need to be right. Explore that need and see what surfaces. How can I bring more peace into the situation?

Ponderings

Five Love Languages (W)

I've had numerous discussions throughout my coaching career with folks who feel their parents did not love them, or did not love them in a manner that expressed their love clearly. Learning about the "five love languages," as described by Gary Chapman, has greatly expanded my understanding of what it means to love. Mr. Chapman lists them as follows:

- Words of affirmation
- Acts of service
- Physical touch
- Receiving gifts
- Quality time spent together

I am a baby-boomer. In general, we boomers were raised by a generation who held that providing for their family (acts of service) was love in action. If you were well cared for, had your basic needs met, then the rest (the other four love languages) was bonus, not necessary. Our parents were raised by people who felt the same way—it was all our parents knew.

Typically each of us has one primary love language. Consider the parents, partner and children in your life. Is the relationship a smooth one or tumultuous one? It is worth considering what the other person's primary love language is. Is it the same as yours? My husband and I have the same love language (acts of service), and we've had a long-term, loving, mostly peaceful relationship. With this list of love languages, you can see that if there's a mismatch in love languages, some effort at compromise is in order, or there's bound to be some frustration.

These love languages are a powerful tool for understanding relationships, increasing love and parenting. Please investigate further. There is a quiz you can take to determine your primary love language. You can read more about Gary Chapman's work and books and take the quiz at 5lovelanguages.com.

"If we are to develop an intimate relationship, we need to know each other's desires. If we wish to love each other, we need to know what the other person wants. The good news is that all of the five love languages can be learned." Gary Chapman

To Ponder: What is my primary love language (don't guess, take the quiz)? Do I feel loved? What is the primary love language of those closest to me? How can I use this information to better understand my relationships and make improvements if needed?

Ponderings

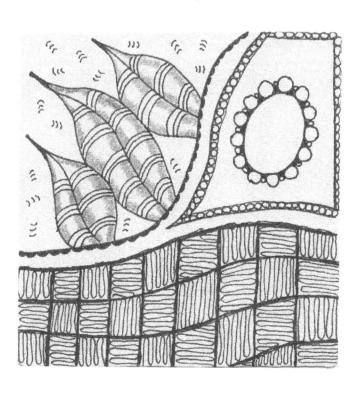

What If? (W)

Here I offer some "what if" questions to inspire you to consider some commonly-held beliefs.

What if we are not meant to suffer here?

What if life is supposed to be easy and you are designed for happiness?

What if there is no such thing as the devil or hell?

What if we are not sinners, but glorious creations of Spirit loved eternally and infinitely?

What if you create your life by how you think?

What if there's no judgment when we die?

What if you are completely responsible for your body and all you experience in it, including disease?

What if abundance (in all forms) is truly unlimited, and there is enough for all?

What if you stayed out of other people's business?

What if we felt kinship rather than separation from those in "other" groups (religions, nationalities, sexual orientation, etc.)?

What if what you believe really isn't serving you, and doesn't feel true to your heart?

What if we really do have an inner guidance system that leads us lovingly every step of the way?

What if you were free to say "yes" or "no" and really mean it, without justification?

What if being true to yourself is more important than how much you accomplish?

These are big questions. Pick one to ponder, and come back here later if you'd like to tackle another. Your beliefs relative to each of these questions has a profound effect on the way you live your life, so reflecting on them is assuredly time well spent.

"What if everything is an illusion and nothing exists? In that case, I definitely overpaid for my carpet." Woody Allen

To Ponder: What am I learning about myself and my beliefs as I ponder these questions?

Ponderings

Shame (W/H)

"You should be ashamed of yourself." I'd venture to say that we have all had these words spoken at us at least one time in our lives. We may have even repeated them to ourselves.

We all feel shame at some point. It is grossly unpleasant. It makes us feel isolated, vulnerable, flawed, less than human. We tend to stuff this unpleasant emotion away in some bodily "closet" where we hope no one can see it. Unfortunately this perpetuates the shame. Our best bet to overcome shame is to share it in a safe place and release it.

Here's a shame story that affected much of my adult life. This occurred on Christmas morning when I was about eight years old. We had opened our gifts, and I was checking under the tree to see if we had retrieved all of them. I innocently said, "Is that all there is?" I meant, did we find all of them? I was not feeling in any way that we hadn't received enough stuff. Alas, my dad interpreted my question the wrong way, and verbally tore into me, shaming me for my ingratitude. I was shocked, having been so misinterpreted. I felt horrible, and it ruined my Christmas. I also vowed to myself from that point on that I would not speak spontaneously ever again—I would be extremely careful in choosing my every word.

It took a lot of years (decades) for me to be willing to share this story, and quite a bit of spiritual support to get over the shame of the event. It has been a long-term practice for me to allow myself to speak freely and spontaneously. It's not easy to open up and release shame, but it is so freeing to drop that baggage.

"Shame cannot survive being spoken...and being met with empathy." Brene Brown

To Ponder: I recognize this as a safe place. Below is a shame story I am ready to release. How might my behavior change for having released this shame?

Ponderings

Keep Moving (H)

Word has it nowadays in the scientific community that sitting is the new smoking. This means that frequent and prolonged sitting is as bad for your health as smoking. That's distressing, but also hopefully motivational news. I expect this confirms what desk-jobbers and couch potatoes have inherently known for quite some time. It is also important to note that physical movement supports not only your body, but also your mind. It is essential to a healthy vibrant brain.

While an exercise regimen is helpful in combating the effects of sitting, it's not the primary answer. That answer is: get up and move, often. Many folks have not found an exercise "plan" that suits them, for whatever reason. This does not keep you from moving your body.

Even with a "desk job," there are ways to avoid sitting. There are desks that move up and down, so that you can stand and work. Suggest meetings where folks stand instead of sit—that may shorten meetings considerably, a double blessing. Modern technology enables us to work in many different environments, even outside. Most folks would agree that even if you are sitting outside, being outside is better than inside. And you had to move to get out there.

How can you incorporate more movement into your day? All change starts with awareness, simply noticing how much you sit. I'm lucky enough to work from home, so I get up from my desk often to do a task, such as put laundry in the dryer, empty the dishwasher, or walk to the mailbox. House-cleaning is an excellent (though not my favorite) way to get moving. Mow your own lawn. Plant a garden, and then keep it neatly tended. Walk to a friend's house. If you must work at an office, take frequent stretching breaks. Even arms overhead with side bends is an energizing move. Step outside and breathe deeply. Go get a glass of water (few folks drink enough water). Walk over and speak to someone instead of emailing or texting. Once you set the intention to sit less and move more, ideas for movement will come.

"You don't get the ass you want by sitting on it." Anonymous

To Ponder: Do I sit a lot in a typical day? How can I incorporate more movement into my day? What are my favorite ways to move my body?

Ponderings

35-Minute Heart-Opener (O)

Please don't skip this exercise. It will help you navigate through the rest of this adventure with a clearer picture of what matters to you. Even if you have done this exercise before, do it again, because <u>you</u> are different now from when you previously did it.

Set aside the noted time to be uninterrupted, including devices. It would be helpful, however, to have a timer. A three-minute egg timer is just right. Also, you'll need paper and a writing instrument to make notes.

In the first three minutes, make a list of the 10 things that you value most in life. There are no right or wrong inclusions, it is your list. Put "carrot cake" on there if you want. It's a list of what makes your life special to you.

In the next three-minute slot, cross one thing off the list, the one on the list you can most stand to give up. It is now gone from your life, permanently. Take pen to paper and write about how that feels. This is not a literary work of art, just record your feelings and thoughts. Words, pictures, phrases, scribbles—all are fine.

In the remaining nine three-minute time slots, repeat the cross-off-one-item-and-journal process. After you've let go of everything important to you, spend as much time as you need with the feelings and thoughts, recording on paper whatever you feel you'd like to note.

"It's not hard to make decisions once you know what your values are." Roy E. Disney

To Ponder: How was this exercise valuable to me?

<u>Ponderings</u>

Personal Manifesto (W/H/O/A)

A manifesto is "a written statement declaring publicly the intentions, motives, or views of its issuer." (Merriam-Webster dictionary) I was in a workshop a few years ago and the presenter had us write our own personal manifesto. He explained that it is not only a statement of beliefs, but also a creative document stating your intention of how you choose to live. It is important that it be written in the present tense, as you intend life to be <u>now</u>, not in some far-off someday.

A manifesto is deeply personal. You will note in my manifesto below that Q is my nickname for my higher power, and "spiritual shove" is my affectionate term for Q's endless encouragement to get me to do something great. Here's my manifesto:

> I trust Q and I trust myself. I live my vision of "<u>W</u>hole heart connection." I am a creative conduit for Spirit in the world. I am responsible for my happiness and I am happy. Every day is a gift. I am wildly beloved and abundantly blessed in every way. I receive graciously. I lead a charmed life. I practice living in a healthy manner. I am reliable. I continually seek to reveal the potency of my spiritual nature. I am heaven. I am inspired and I inspire. I love a good "spiritual shove" and bringing a new adventure or creation to life. Knowing that life flows in divine order and divine timing is all I need to know.

Even after a few years have passed, this still fits me and feels good when I read it. Be sure to read it out loud to "test" it, as that helps to check the fit. When it's just the way you want it, you'll know it. It will feel pleasing to your inner self. It doesn't matter what anyone else says about it. The presenter critiqued my manifesto and said I should change some things, and I said, "It's mine, not yours, and I like it the way it is. It is meaningful to me, and that's all that matters." Be creative. Write down lots of ideas. Move things around. Play with words. It's a fun and powerful spiritual project.

"We either live with intention or exist by default." Kristin Armstrong

To Ponder: My manifesto…

Ponderings

FUN2BME (W/O)

This title is a vanity license plate I saw a while back in my home state of Kansas. I love it. How joyful is it that someone enjoys being herself so much that she invested in this license plate for her car!

On a recent road trip with several galpals, one raised the challenge of giving her one-word descriptors of herself. The other three of us hopped on the bandwagon with "loving, compassionate, seeker, energetic, traveler" and so on. We later did the exercise for each of us. Only a few words were repeated. We each had a unique set of words painting our portrait. I don't recall that there were any big surprises. It was a joyful, affirming exercise. All of us are mature enough to know who we are, and we're comfortable in our own skin.

This leads me to the idea that we figure out what we want folks to say about us at our funeral, then live so that they will say those things with feeling. I really want people to say that Leta really had fun being Leta. The words that my friends used to describe me are words I would love to have used in reference to me once I've passed. The one-word exercise was also a powerful reminder that we influence those around us much more by our actions, the way we live, than by our words.

"Nothing is more rare, nor more beautiful, than a woman being unapologetically herself; comfortable in her perfect imperfection. To me, that is the true essence of beauty." Steve Maraboli

"Me? Crazy? I should get down off this unicorn and slap you." Anonymous

To Ponder: Collect a few friends and do the one-word exercise. How did it go? Are these words the ones I want used when I am gone from the planet? If not, what words would I prefer?

Ponderings

Be Impeccable with Your Word (A)

This is from a marvelous little book of wisdom called "The Four Agreements" by Don Miguel Ruiz. (All four Agreements are covered in this book.) This is a very powerful practice, as your word is your power to create your life. Your word is a force, and it can cause goodness or destruction to flow from you.

While this may sound easy on initial reading, it is definitely a life-long practice. It requires you to always speak with integrity. This, first and foremost, applies to yourself. Never speaking a word of criticism or negativity towards yourself? Now, that's a challenge, but with the greatest rewards. It is only by using your word lovingly with yourself that you are able to extend love to others.

Using your word in judgment, blame or guilt against another is also a break of impeccability and poor reflection on yourself. Your word is like a seed, and once planted in another, can grow into something lovely, or into "weeds." One example of this is my dad's proclamation to me as a youngster, "There is no musical talent in the Miller family." Having no basis to dispute, I took that in, and have not put any effort into developing any musical talent that may be latent in me, as early on, I proved him correct by "failing" a choir audition.

Always speak the truth. Yikes! I don't lie, you say, but do you always tell the whole truth? Just look at the comical question, "Do these pants make my butt look fat?" and you'll recall multiple instances where you thought it safer not to speak the whole truth.

Perhaps the worst example of not being impeccable with your word is gossip. Mr. Ruiz refers to gossip as "pure poison." It is extremely pervasive in our communication. It can forever taint relationships and interactions. It is addictive, and can be an extremely tough habit to break. Gossip is truly a violent act both toward oneself and the subject of gossip.

By the way, this Agreement applies to one's thoughts as well as to one's spoken words.

Mr. Ruiz offers this result of practicing this Agreement: "Impeccability of the word can lead you to personal freedom, to huge success and abundance; it can take away all fear and transform it into joy and love."

"How much you love yourself and how you feel about yourself are directly proportionate to the quality and integrity of your word." Don Miguel Ruiz

To Ponder: How do I use my word, both toward myself and others? Is it impeccable? If not, how might I change it? Do I gossip? How might I lessen this damaging use of my word?

Ponderings

Slow Medicine

This is the title of a book by Michael Finkelstein, M.D. I highly recommend it as a guided in-depth exploration of one's health, using the author's 77 Questions for Skillful Living. Dr. Finkelstein, via his personal experience, discusses how Western medicine is great for acute injuries and minor illnesses, such as broken bones and sinus infections, but it has failed us in coping with chronic illnesses and long-term health issues, especially those related to lifestyle. He takes a "whole person" view of care and treatment, which is nearly impossible to find in today's Western doctor population.

Please understand that I am not placing all the blame for our generally sad state of health on doctors. Much of it falls on lack of responsibility on the part of the patients as well. The general mentality is that folks really don't want to change to get better, they want the doctor to fix it. It's a lose-lose situation.

One of the maddening things I've noticed over my lifetime is that for many folks, if their doctor told them to jump off a cliff, they'd go do just that, no questions asked. The doctor knows best, and they close themselves off to other possibilities. Here's a well-ignored fact: no doctor has ever healed anyone—we all, ultimately, heal ourselves. Our amazing bodies do the healing.

So why not simply work with our bodies, minds and spirits to heal ourselves? The excuses are endless. It takes too long. That's "woowoo." It's not covered by insurance. I don't want to change my diet or exercise or whatever. If I'm taking responsibility, I have no one to blame but myself. I can't find anyone to support my efforts. On and on it goes.

Here's a personal story of slow medicine. For several years I had an ache in my left hip, bearable, but fairly constant. I had unfortunately settled into the mentality of "I'm getting older, I'm gonna hurt somewhere." Occasionally I would take an over-the-counter pain reliever. I maintained my usual activities of swimming, yoga, golf and walking, though the ache limited my walking to a mile at a time. I did not go to the doctor about it, because I knew he would look at my date of birth and say "arthritis." (I've witnessed this too many times in my older-adult yoga student population.) I am extremely opposed to a doctor labeling me with a condition.

At the beginning of 2016, I decided that I'd had enough of the aching and embarked on finding a way to get rid of it. I started with my chiropractor, where I learned my sacrum was out of alignment, and we've cared for that with regular adjustments. Those started out weekly, and now I see her every two or three weeks. That was a beginning in taking care of the structural alignment problem. I also continued my regular monthly massage, focusing on the muscles around the hip.

I followed my intuition frequently on this journey, as well as noting guidance offered to me along the way by others. One of my yoga students told me about Whole 30 (whole30.com), a diet-exploration plan that intrigued me. When I learned in May that another super-health-conscious friend had done the Whole 30 program, I was inspired to do it. It gave me valuable insight into how foods affect my body, with the added bonus that I had 25 fewer pounds for my hip to carry around. This same Whole 30 friend also told me about the Melt Method, a body movement system that works with the fascia, the connective tissue throughout our bodies. In September I began a daily regimen of using the Melt techniques, easy to do in about 20 minutes a day. That has been an incredibly important piece of the healing puzzle, and I can say that I rarely have hip pain anymore. I am up to walking two miles easily again.

However, after years of compensating for the hip pain, the muscles surrounding it, especially in my thigh, are still quite tight. Enter my amazing massage therapist again. I asked her to work on my IT band (muscle running along the outside of the thigh), and she applied kinesiology tape to that. It's the stuff you see on the shoulders of basketball players. Who knew?!?! It has had a huge effect on my leg mobility, stiffness after sitting a while, and muscle tightness. I also learned that I can buy the tape online, and there are videos showing how to apply it to many parts of the body. Another piece of the healing puzzle falls into place. Holy cow, self-care, I love it.

This has been a year-long journey so far. I knew it would not be a quick fix. I've learned a lot of valuable information about myself along the way. I've made changes in what I eat. I've worked hard at maintaining an attitude of health as opposed to illness. No drugs or M.D.s were used in the process. Best of all, my hip rarely hurts anymore, and I'm convinced that if I continue using the techniques I've learned, that my muscles will relax. My body knows what to do if I support its innate healing capabilities. Yours does, too.

'The best "quick fix" for your health, you see, is not a quick fix at all; rather, it is slow medicine—a methodical step-by-step process of asking questions that lead to awareness that turns into action that results in extraordinary health.' Michael Finkelstein

Pitch One Thing Every Day (A)

She who dies with the most stuff, wins. Alas, while our behavior may suggest that we believe this, it is definitely not true.

I had the privilege of traveling in a group of 10 to Uganda in 2005 on a mission trip to build a home in Suubi, a Watoto village (watoto.com). That experience really brought home to me how we Americans are obsessed with unnecessary stuff. We built a simple brick home for a widowed mother and eight orphans, the placement set-up for Watoto. There were many other homes already occupied, so we were blessed to interact with the "families." They have shelter, clothing, education, food and the equipment to cook and eat it. There wasn't much beyond that, and they are extremely happy people.

Come back around the world to the U.S. Storage units are popping up seemingly everywhere to store our stuff. Folks are in overwhelming credit card debt due to buying toys and stuff to "keep up with the Joneses." There's even a newly-labeled addiction, hoarding. People collect stuff to the point of obsession, and are traumatized when anyone wants to take away their stuff. We've all heard horror stories of houses so full, there are only narrow paths to move around. We live the attitude, "if some is good, more is better." We are crippling ourselves in so many ways with our over-accumulation of stuff.

You can most likely look around yourself this instant and find some clutter. Clutter is messy, sure, but it is also mentally and spiritually disconcerting. It annoys us, we can't find what we need—it's the "messy desk, messy mind" syndrome. If you've ever tidied away some clutter, you know how good it feels.

I'm inviting you to go one step further. Pitch one thing every day. Trash or donation, up to you. Don't bring anything into your home that's not consumable. Lighten the load for yourself and your heirs. Make your physical space and mental space more open.

"In the real world, what matters is who you are, not what you have." Anonymous

To Ponder: What am I willing to pitch? What do I buy—more things or more consumables? Do I really need more non-consumable things? What chores does my stuff require me to do (such as storing or dusting)? Keep adding to the pitch list and pitching.

Ponderings

Simple Prayer (W/A)

Whether or not we believe in something bigger than ourselves, we occasionally throw out a request for help into the ethers, into the unknown. We may or may not believe that something hears us and answers us. We may be convinced that something is a nice entity or nasty. We may call it God, Higher Power, Big Life or Ralph. Names don't matter. My nickname for it is "Q." Q and I have a lively relationship.

I was taught a version of prayer known as affirmative prayer. It states the desired outcome in the present tense, as already received and complete, rather than requesting something be delivered off in the future.

Here's a very simple version: God is good, so am I, all is well, thanks, goodbye.

I choose to recognize the divine as a benevolent presence (God is good). This is certainly more uplifting and hopeful than the alternative. I am created from divine substance, so I am good also (so am I). What more do I want in life than "all is well"? I seal it with gratitude for all goodness (thanks), and close (goodbye). Prayers can develop into flowery verbiage and lengthy requests, but this simple prayer takes care of everything quite nicely.

I like to use this prayer especially when I'm feeling anxious, for instance, during takeoff and landing in an airplane. It is an excellent and easy prayer to teach to children. It is also useful prior to an anticipated difficult interaction. This simple prayer and a few deep breaths can make your life flow much easier.

"Prayer clears the mist and brings back peace to the Soul." Rumi

To Ponder: How can I use this simple prayer? With whom can I share it?

Ponderings

An Ugly Situation (O/A)

A friend or family member has become embroiled in a relationship which you believe is not in the person's best interest. You may feel he or she is being used or abused or taken advantage of financially. The ugly possibilities are seemingly endless. You are worried and want to help, but you don't know how. The urge to fix the situation is strong within you. Why can't your friend see what's happening!?!? Have you ever experienced this situation?

If you've ever tried to wade into such a situation with fixing in mind, I expect the results were not rewarding. You probably made a mental "note to self" not to attempt such a rescue again.

Everyone here on Playground Earth is experiencing the benefit of free will, the ability to choose for themselves. While we may think some folks aren't so good at using their free will, nevertheless, we must allow everyone to make their own choices. We certainly don't want anyone messing with our use of free will, so why do we feel we should interfere with others?

OK, so we let the friend make his or her choices. We want to be supportive and loving, but we still don't like the situation. What can we do?

Absorb these wise words from Esther Hicks:

> **"You will know when you are of value to anyone when you are able to think about the person and feel good at the same time. When you love others without worry, you are an advantage to them. When you enjoy them, you help them. When you expect them to succeed, you help them. In other words, when you see them as your own Inner Being sees them, then and only then is your association with them to their advantage."** Abraham-Hicks

Your thoughts about the situation contribute to the situation. Do you want to add goodness or negativity to it? Use your own free will to bring love to the "ugly" situation, and you may find that it ends up not so ugly.

To Ponder: Do I relate to the ugly situation? Have I tried to fix one? What were the results? What did I learn? How can I change my thinking about such a situation to be more loving and supportive?

Ponderings

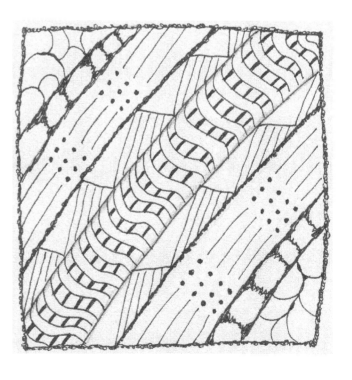

Inner Shirley (A)

Today's exploration is dedicated to my wonderful mother-in-law, Shirley. She has a very powerful talent for selecting exactly the right words to handle a difficult or "sticky" situation. She would have made an outstanding diplomat. I've often said that she could cut you to shreds and you'd beg for more. She is that good with words.

Knowing we've all been in at least one "sticky" situation, I expect we also know the results of using the "right" or "wrong" words to deal with it. It is an exceedingly valuable use of time to ponder the words that will gracefully achieve your desired outcome. Her son, my husband, and I refer to this as accessing our "Inner Shirley."

What are the characteristics of "Inner Shirley" statements? Words are delivered in a calm and unemotional manner. They are stated clearly. It's a "just the facts, ma'am" delivery. It's all spoken from the speaker's point of view. There is no dragging the listener through the mud or criticizing the listener. Words are spoken with confidence and grace, a gentle knowing that these carefully chosen words will achieve the desired outcome. No lie is ever spoken.

A classic example from Shirley herself is her response to annoying telemarketer calls. She says, in a very distressed voice, "You had no way of knowing this, but you've called at a very bad time." They usually apologize and hang up.

"Diplomacy is the art of letting somebody else have your way." David Frost

To Ponder: What difficult situation do I need to resolve? Using the characteristics of "Inner Shirley" statements above, what do I want to say? Practice. Ask for review by a trusted friend before delivery. Let my "Inner Shirley" gracefully resolve the situation. Describe the experience.

Ponderings

Where You Live (A)

My husband and I often discuss the things we love about living in Wichita. With all the negativity in the news, it's a nice change of focus.

I love that it's easy to get around by car, as opposed to a bigger city. We have great art around the city, as well as an outstanding art museum. Theater is abundant with lots of variety. Downtown, especially along the river, has been transformed into a landscape of beauty. Our Old Town district is hopping. We have a lot of great locally-owned restaurants and brewpubs. Folks smile a lot here. We have a great park system and many miles of bicycle trails. Our botanical garden and zoo are both world-class attractions. It's easy to find some variety of live music on any given night. We have several fine universities, supporting educational, cultural and artistic diversity. The cost of living is quite reasonable. It gets cold enough in the winter to kill the bugs. It's comfortable to live here.

This is a fun exercise. Wherever you live, it surely has lots going for it, if only you'll notice. If not, maybe it's time to move, but remember, if you do that, you're taking you with you.

"We don't stop playing because we grow old; we grow old because we stop playing."
George Bernhard Shaw

To Ponder: What are the benefits, pleasures and attractions where I live? What can I do to enjoy my home area more fully?

Ponderings

Worry (H/A)

In a fear-based culture such as that of the U.S., it is seen as extremely natural to worry. So natural, in fact, that many folks think if you don't worry, there's something wrong with you. Nevertheless, worrying is a choice.

Worry causes so much needless distress and wasted energy. Generally the subject of concern doesn't come about anyway. How often, for example, have your worried about your own or someone else's travels, only to have all arrive safe and sound? Worry takes your focus into the future, wherein you miss the joys of the present moment.

Dedicated worriers believe that their worrying efforts indicate their level of love and concern for the target of their worries. Alas, the target probably isn't worrying and doesn't know about nor need those efforts. There are much better ways to support others than worrying. (See **An Ugly Situation**, p. 136.)

One remedy for worrying is to ask what's the worst that could happen? And how likely is it? Yes, a meteor could hit the earth and we'll all die, but that's not really likely. Often when we stop long enough to really consider these questions, we find that disaster is not really imminent, and we can stop worrying.

Another consideration relative to worry is to note one's desire to control a situation, accompanied by no ability whatsoever to do so. It's certainly a frustrating spot to be in. However, instead of self-damaging worry, mentally hold the participants and situation in love and know that something bigger than you is in charge. It is, the bigger that makes stars and such. This is a good thing and a big relief.

You'll be amazed what all that worrying energy can do when put to creative use.

"What worries you masters you." Haddon W. Robinson

To Ponder: What am I worried about at the moment? What's the worst that could happen? Is that likely? Is my worrying helping the situation? What other choice do I have?

Ponderings

Drop the Resistance (W)

We come here to playground Earth to create a life. With our free will and innate power to create, we truly can create the life of our dreams. Many don't do that, however. There's a lot of resistance, and all of it comes from within. What forms does that resistance take?

A huge form of resistance is the idea that others can, but not me, that I am somehow different and not endowed with the same life energy as everyone else. This shows up in various ways: others may be cured, but not me; I'm too old, young, stupid, (fill in the blank); I can't do it perfectly, so why bother.

Another form of resistance we use is allowing labels to define us and how we live in the world. Labels can come from doctors (you have "chronic xyz"), family members and teachers (you're no good at "abc"), society (your background or ethnicity means you won't accomplish much).

Resistance also shows up in the mentality that someday things will be different, that eventually we'll have the time or money or energy to do, be or have what we want. This is a resistant attitude because it keeps you focused on the future, and you lose the creativity of the present, the only place you can create a different life.

Probably the ultimate form of resistance to life is a belief in your own unworthiness. Your life is a direct reflection of how you value yourself. If you don't believe you are worthy of a good life, you'll likely not be active in pursuing one. Actually, that's what this book is about—exploring your beliefs and actions and using tools to expand your consciousness of self-appreciation.

"Most of us have two lives: the life we live, and the unlived life within us. Between the two stands Resistance." Steven Pressfield

To Ponder: Do I recognize any of these forms of resistance in my life? How are they affecting me? What might I accomplish if I dropped the resistance?

Ponderings

Don't Make Assumptions (A)

This is another Agreement from the book called "The Four Agreements" by Don Miguel Ruiz. (All four Agreements are covered in this book.)

Don't make assumptions. Are you kidding me?!?!? That's impossible! We do it all the time, it seems like such a natural, organic behavior. We make assumptions about what others are thinking or doing. We see what we want to see, and we hear what we want to hear. We dream up stuff that has no basis in reality. We create drama. Assumptions can truly lead to chaos, especially if we add the poison of gossip to our assumptions.

If you are in a long-term relationship, chances are exceedingly good you have said or thought the phrase relative to your partner, "You should have known…" This is rooted in the assumption that he or she knows you well enough to read your mind. Begging for trouble, that is. I have been married for several decades, and there have been a multitude of times wherein what I was dreaming up in my head about my partner was not even remotely close to reality. A 12-step phrase for making assumptions is the "magic magnifying mind."

We make assumptions because we are afraid to ask questions and to state what we want. Asking questions and creating clear communication are the antidotes to making assumptions. I can't stress this enough: you always have the right to ask. Keep on asking until the subject at hand is clear and assumption-free for all involved. Clear understanding on everyone's part feels good and enables us to be our true selves.

"It is always better to ask questions than to make an assumption, because assumptions set us up for suffering." Don Miguel Ruiz

To Ponder: What assumptions do I make? What questions could eliminate those assumptions? Am I afraid to ask? What's that about? What needs am I having difficulty stating?

Ponderings

Are You a Rule-Follower? (A)

There's a saying from Katharine Hepburn: If you obey all the rules, you miss all the fun. Alas, I am a rule-follower, meaning I generally do as I'm told, though as I've aged and realized that I have that tendency, I've made an effort to be less rigid about rules.

Rule-followers tend to acquire the tendency early on in life. My childhood was fairly unsettled, with verbal abuse, trauma, and addiction. It became my primary mission early on in life to keep my mother happy, so I made every effort to be a "good girl"—don't rock the boat, get good grades, go to church, don't get near trouble of any sort. Following the rules was my way to attempt to control my world which was way out of control. Rules meant order, order meant safety and security. Following rules helped me with my overwhelming mission, or so I thought.

There's nothing wrong with being a rule-follower. Everyone is a rule-follower to some extent, otherwise traffic would be total chaos. We do need rules and people to follow them.

I write about rule-following so that we can be aware of this tendency and the accompanying need to control that which is generally not controllable. For instance, it was an unwritten rule in our home when I was growing up that emotional outbursts of any kind would not be tolerated. Continual squelching of emotions in childhood led me to food addiction and years of recovery that have enabled me to identify and express emotions.

Another characteristic of rule-followers is that they tend to not question the rules. An example of this can be found in a multitude of religions, where participants are given a set of dogma to accept, live by and uphold without question, otherwise, you're not welcome.

Rule-following behavior can indicate some areas in life where we are holding ourselves back from living our full potential. It's worth considering…

"I am free because I know that I alone am morally responsible for everything I do. I am free, no matter what rules surround me. If I find them tolerable, I tolerate them; if I find them too obnoxious, I break them." Robert Heinlein

To Ponder: Am I a rule-follower? How does that show up in my life? Is it holding me back from something I desire? What rule could I safely break to give myself a taste of freedom?

Ponderings

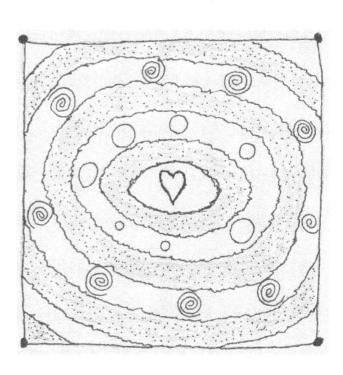

Problem with Food? (H)

The subject of food addiction is near and dear to my heart, as I have had a glorious life due to decades of recovery from it. It is also, ultimately, what put my mother in her grave, as she was a long-term practicing bulimic. Food addiction is a killing disease. It's not a matter of moral failure or insufficient willpower.

Yes, everyone eats too much now and then. Sometimes we don't eat when stressed, even though we're hungry. Overeating is socially acceptable behavior, even encouraged by our ever-enlarging restaurant portion sizes. We <u>have</u> to eat. The problem comes in when we repeatedly practice behaviors with food that take food out of the realm of simple nourishment and into the realm of obsession.

The Overeaters Anonymous website (oa.org) offers "Fifteen Questions" designed to help you evaluate your relationship with food. Here are those questions for you to ponder:

> Do I eat when I'm not hungry, or not eat when my body needs nourishment?
> Do I go on eating binges for no apparent reason, sometimes eating until I'm stuffed or even feel sick?
> Do I have feelings of guilt, shame, or embarrassment about my weight or the way I eat?
> Do I eat sensibly in front of others and then make up for it when I am alone?
> Is my eating affecting my health or the way I live my life?
> When my emotions are intense — whether positive or negative — do I find myself reaching for food?
> Do my eating behaviors make me or others unhappy?
> Have I ever used laxatives, vomiting, diuretics, excessive exercise, diet pills, shots or other medical interventions (including surgery) to try to control my weight?
> Do I fast or severely restrict my food intake to control my weight?
> Do I fantasize about how much better life would be if I were a different size or weight?
> Do I need to chew or have something in my mouth all the time: food, gum, mints, candies or beverages?
> Have I ever eaten food that is burned, frozen or spoiled; from containers in the grocery store or out of the garbage?
> Are there certain foods I can't stop eating after having the first bite?
> Have I lost weight with a diet or "period of control" only to be followed by bouts of uncontrolled eating and/or weight gain?
> Do I spend too much time thinking about food, arguing with myself about whether or what to eat, planning the next diet or exercise cure, or counting calories?

The turning point for me was learning that I was not alone, that there were other people who were just as obsessed about food as I was. I learned through them that life is possible without excess food and the obsession that goes with it. My recovery journey has been, hands down, the best thing that ever happened to me. It has given me freedom from food, an intimate relationship with a higher power, and a life of fulfilling relationships and joy.

"When you believe in yourself more than you believe in food, you will stop using food as if it were your only chance at not falling apart." Geneen Roth

Ponderings

=====Story=====Story=====Story=====Story=====Story=====

The Love and Sadness of My Mom

My mother adored me from day one, no doubt in my mind. I was born 16 years after Arlie, 14 years after Ken, and although I was a "surprise" to my dad and brothers, I don't believe my mother was surprised at all. She lived for her children, and when there was the impending doom of no kids in the home, she did what she could to fill that potential void. Thus, the princess was born.

I truly believe my mom was in heaven those first few years of my life. All was right in her world, for she had the brown-eyed baby girl she'd always wanted. She and Dad took loving care of me. We weren't rich, but we had everything we needed. My dad worked hard every day at the family business, a sawmill in central Pennsylvania. I don't remember much from my earliest years.

Then tragedy struck our family. We were often treated to the use of a distant relative's rustic cabin in north-central Pennsylvania. One weekend in July, my mom went there with the whole family, but she <u>really</u> did not want to be there, too rustic for her, with an outhouse and all. While we were there, my grandmother, her mother, died suddenly of a massive heart attack back at her own home. I don't remember the ensuing chaos or service, just the horrendous after-effects. My mom was devastated, as she was extremely close to her mom. And alas, she blamed her mother's death on my dad, because if he hadn't "made" her go to the cabin, her mother wouldn't have died. I never said this story would make sense!

At four years old, I became terrified. If my grandma could die so suddenly, what was to prevent that from happening to my mom? Mom was so mired in grief that she was emotionally unavailable for years to come. Blaming my dad for her mother's death only hastened the deterioration of their relationship, and I believe, encouraged my dad's turning to alcohol to escape. Looking back, it seemed that Mom settled into the anger stage of grief, and spent an enormous amount of energy suppressing it.

Mom never worked outside the home. She took excellent care of her five-bedroom house, huge garden and roses. She was an outstanding cook, baker, seamstress and knitter. She canned or froze all of her bountiful garden's produce. She even made braided rugs. She was a very talented woman.

Food and love were synonymous with her—the more you ate, the more she loved you. In my efforts to keep her happy (and therefore prevent her from dying like Grandma), that's what I did, I ate. And ate. And ate. And eventually peaked out at about 280 pounds.

When I was in my early 30s, I began recovery from food addiction. It was then that so much about my mother became shockingly clear. I remembered that she ate just as much as I did, including late night "snacks" such as a batch of fried chicken livers or a huge bowl of cereal, but she didn't gain weight. Then I remembered that I would sometimes hear her throwing up after a meal. When I asked her about it, she'd say her "stomach was just upset." Bingo! The light came on for me. She was a practicing bulimic, a full-blown food addict herself. She had all the symptoms of bulimia, including dental, heart and liver complications.

I truly believe that she felt that she had found a convenient way to eat as much as she wanted without gaining weight. Back then, overeating was socially acceptable, even encouraged, and certainly not a sign of any problem. She had to have some means of coping with her grief, her unhappy marriage and rampant codependency. She did have some inner inkling that things weren't right, however, because she would spend hours reading her two-volume medical encyclopedia, trying to figure out what was wrong with her.

My life has been completely blessed by having access to recovery from addiction, and practicing that recovery on a daily basis. My mom didn't have that option. She didn't know she had the illness of compulsive eating. Even if she had known, there was no help available at that time, especially in the boondocks of Pennsylvania. And as upset as she was with my dad's drinking, she would likely never have accepted the fact that she, too, was an addict.

Recognizing all this has led me to release the anger and disappointment I once felt towards her. I've replaced it with compassion, for her ability to love me and the rest of her family as best she could, despite the huge, undiagnosed handicap of addiction. She passed at the early age of 61 from liver cancer. Though it doesn't say so on her death certificate, I firmly believe that it was the long-term bulimia practice that destroyed her liver and took her life.

I am so grateful that resources are now readily available to rescue addicts from these downward spirals. No one needs to suffer any longer as my mother did much of her life.

Suffering (W)

Our free will is the source of our suffering. Suffering is a choice. We have complete free will—nothing is imposed on us from the outside unless we agree to it. As human beings, we tend to operate in very short-sighted, instant gratification mode. In the midst of a period of suffering, we often look outside ourselves for something or someone to make it stop. We think it may go on forever, forgetting that we have been through similar periods in the past, survived and realized a greater degree of life experience as a result.

We are the ones who save ourselves from suffering. It's all in the attitude we hold toward the situation. If we see the situation as part of the flow of life, not judging it as "bad," looking for the blessing that is most definitely included, we can pass through periods of upheaval without suffering.

One place I regularly encounter suffering is having my yoga students do abdominal work. While I'll grant that few folks actually enjoy doing abs, suffering is not necessary, as the results of core work are very desirable. I tell them before we even start, "Turn off your suffering-o-meter."

Another way to look at suffering is via the common phrase, "what goes around comes around." Simply put, anything we do to another, we do to ourselves. We cannot hurt someone without hurting ourselves at the same time. Conversely, we cannot hurt ourselves (suffering) without hurting others, because when we are down on ourselves, we are not giving our best self to the world. An alternate way to state this is that we are not punished *for* our actions, but *by* them. We experience the consequences of our actions here and now, not at some future time in eternity. Otherwise, how would we learn? I would suggest that the reason so many people appear to have "run amok" in our world is because they believe there are no personal and immediate consequences to their actions. That simply cannot be in a universe where we are all aspects of one unified whole.

We will experience pain in life, physical, emotional and mental. It's part of the human experience. Suffering, however, is optional.

"Suffering usually relates to wanting things to be different from the way they are." Allan Lokos

To Ponder: Under what circumstances have I suffered? What choices were available to me? How could I have chosen differently to lessen the suffering?

Ponderings

Do You Really Want to Be Healed? (H)

I'm a recovering addict. In the 12-step programs, the only requirement for membership is a desire to stop using your addictive substance or behavior. In our culture run by insurance companies and big pharma, we have manifested myriad chronic conditions such as chronic fatigue and fibromyalgia. Poor eating and sleeping habits create even more health problems.

I've seen firsthand both in myself and other addicts the desire to have the effects of the addiction gone while still being able to indulge in our chosen substances or behaviors. Who doesn't want the effects of a chronic condition relieved without having to change in any way? Ah, there's the key. We really don't want to have to go through the seemingly huge effort of changing our lifestyle for relief.

Then there's another complication. We've become adept at using our condition to gain attention and to manipulate others. Note right now that these are most likely unconscious behaviors, but they are used nonetheless. Here's an example. For a person who has trouble saying 'no,' it can be oh, so convenient to say she can't do something because of a condition flair-up. The condition or addiction can easily become a handy control mechanism.

Hence, my initial question… do you really want to be healed? Healing only ever happens when the consequences of the addiction or condition become worse than the benefits gained. If you really explore deeply, you'll see that there is some payback to a chronic condition, or the person wouldn't be hanging onto it so tightly.

This can be a truly "in your face" question. I've been there. I spent years of my life wanting to eat more than I wanted to be healthy. If this question irritates you, that's a good thing. It's stirring something within you. If nothing else, I hope it makes you more aware of the behaviors of folks with addictions or chronic conditions. Healing is a choice.

"Healing takes courage, and we all have courage, even if we have to dig a little to find it."
Tori Amos

To Ponder: Do I have a chronic condition or practice an addiction? What benefit(s) do I get from it? Are they worth it? How do I use my condition or addiction to influence others?

Ponderings

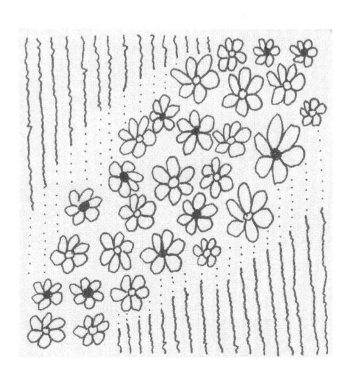

It's OK to Not Watch the News (A)

As I write this, the 2016 presidential election is just a few weeks behind us, and the negativity in the news from all sides is truly unprecedented. With most of the news designed to incite rather than report, there's no confidence in anything being fact or true anymore. So, yes, it's OK to not get sucked into all this.

Certainly we want to be informed citizens. But at what cost? Particularly if you are an empath, taking in all this negativity can be damaging to your physical and/or psychological health. Even if you are not empathic, all this negativity, questionable reporting and drama can leave you completely frustrated and rapidly losing hope.

It's OK to unplug. The amount of information available to us these days is beyond overwhelming, and we don't have to know it all, thank goodness. Can you trust that, just for today, you'll learn what you need to learn? That the world will continue turning if you are not mired in the news? That focusing on the positive, reaching for one better-feeling thought, will enable you to more fully enjoy life?

How do you unplug? Put down that electronic device and pick up a book and read it instead. Only watch the news once or twice a week. Use your news-consuming time to take a walk or have a conversation with someone you love. Check social media, if you must, only once a day. Look only to a source you trust for news and ignore the others. Seek out inspiring news, such as that provided by upworthy.com. Only you can change your view of the world.

"Headlines, in a way, are what mislead you because bad news is a headline, and gradual improvement is not." Bill Gates

To Ponder: Does the news get me down? Do I really need to indulge in so much drama? What one step can I take to disengage from the negativity? What next step?

Ponderings

The Right to Ask (A)

It is an extremely essential skill in life to be able to ask for what you need and want. It's born within us—it's why babies cry—they need something, and it's their way of asking. It is a natural, organic behavior. Unfortunately, social conditioning, poor parenting and life events have a way of squelching this natural ability. As we squelch the ability to ask, we gradually lose touch with our needs and wants, and life falls into survival mode.

One reason we don't ask is because we don't want to bother anyone. Another is the mistaken belief that our needs aren't really that important. We may simply be afraid that the answer will not be what we want. We may have been conditioned to be seen and not heard (an extremely common social conditioning, especially prevalent among women). If we ask for what we want and receive it, then we'll be indebted to the person and "owe" them something in return. The excuses for not asking are endless.

Being able and willing to ask is a sign of thriving. It is a sign of strength, not weakness. In The Four Agreements, Don Miguel Ruiz puts it this way: "Find your voice to ask for what you want. Everybody has the right to tell you no or yes, but you always have the right to ask. Likewise, everybody has the right to ask you, and you have the right to say yes or no."

"Everything you want is out there waiting for you to ask. Everything you want also wants you. But you have to take action to get it." Jules Renard

To Ponder: What am I needing or wanting to ask for? Do it. How did it feel? What were the results? What is next in my asking practice?

Ponderings

Self-Care Is Not Optional (H/A)

I probably ought to repeat this heading in all capital letters, but that would seem like yelling. That's how strongly I feel about this topic of self-care. It is so important and so often neglected.

The common arguments against self-care are just plain ridiculous. "It's selfish." That's stated by people who want your time selfishly for themselves. It is NOT selfish (yes, I'm yelling) to take care of yourself. "I don't have time." Very simply, we invest time in what we value. If you say you don't have time for self-care, you are plainly stating that you are not worth the time. Is that the message you want to exemplify, especially to your children? "I don't even know what would make me feel good." C'mon, you are perfectly capable of figuring out how to care for yourself. It's a practice, like all of life.

Set aside some time for yourself to be undisturbed, putting an event in your calendar if need be. Get away from those who make demands on you. List at least three things that you can do on a daily, weekly and monthly basis to care for yourself. These do not have to be huge, time-consuming tasks. Here are examples from my list:

Daily… Get sunshine on my skin, floss teeth, write in my journal

Weekly… Talk with my prayer partner, attend a 12-step meeting, call my sons

Monthly… See a movie in the theater, have a pedicure, have a massage

I find it a good practice to review the list daily to check off those items I did. It is important to use the list for self-observation, not for self-criticism.

The ideal approach to self-care is to be your own best friend. You would not discourage a friend from taking care of herself, so don't devalue yourself that way.

"Growing into your future with health and grace and beauty doesn't have to take all your time. It rather requires a dedication to caring for yourself as if you were rare and precious, which you are, and regarding all life around you as equally so, which it is."
Victoria Moran

To Ponder: Set aside uninterrupted time and create a daily/weekly/monthly self-care list. Keep it handy, observe, adjust the list as needed. What challenges my ability to care for myself? How can I eliminate those challenges, enlist others' support, or change my priorities so that I can more easily love on myself?

Ponderings

Autopilot vs. Aware (A)

We all, to a greater or lesser extent, move through some things in life on autopilot. There are lots of routine things we do in a day that are habits, that we do rather unconsciously. Brushing teeth is an example. Jonathan Fields, author and entrepreneur, suggests that the opposite of an autopilot habit is ritual, which he describes as an intentional, mindful act.

Thriving in life, as opposed to surviving, requires us to spend more time in intentional, mindful ritual than in unconscious habit. We won't eliminate habits, that's not even practical. What we are seeking is more mindfulness in ordinary actions. That means actually paying attention to what we are doing. Not only is this good for the actual completion of the task, but it is also an excellent way to support mental sharpness.

A simple way to restore present-moment awareness is to take a few full breaths, paying attention to what it feels like in the body to breathe deeply. This can then take us into focusing on the task in front of us. This is a practice with never-ending potential for skill development.

We can start investigating our level of awareness by simply looking back over the day just completed and seeing how much detail we can remember. If we can't remember much, chances are good we have moved through the day mostly on autopilot.

An excellent place to begin practicing mindfulness is when eating. Eliminate electronic devices, TV, reading materials, any sort of distraction, and sit down and pay attention to the act of eating and the food you are consuming. It's an amazing, enjoyable process if you pay attention to it. It also makes for better digestion and assimilation.

Another great place to practice mindfulness is in a task that's not a favorite. For me, that's housecleaning. I make it more mindful by 1) being grateful that I am physically fit to do it, and 2) dedicating myself to accomplishing as much as I can till my one-hour timer goes off (then I get to stop cleaning). I really have to stay focused to accomplish as much as possible in that one-hour time slot.

Gratitude swells along with our present-moment awareness, and we thrive.

"Walk as if you are kissing the earth with your feet." Anonymous

To Ponder: What task can I do in a more mindful manner? What were the results of changing my focus? Where else can I bring more mindfulness into my day?

Ponderings

Something To Look Forward To (O)

My life is, on the whole, quite wonderful, and the past year was no exception. I usually look with great anticipation into a new year. The beginning of this year, however, found me a) ill for several weeks (quite a rare thing for me), and b) experiencing a clutsy, painful fall. The dragging-on nature of both these things was getting me down.

I don't like to "make a home" in a low place, so I made my reservation at a summer camp for adults: Camp GLP (goodlifeproject.com). This is a big step outside my box, as I hated camp as a kid, being relatively an introvert. But I <u>want</u> to get outside my box. My second move to get out of my low spot was to call my friend in Chicago whom I visit each year for a Cubs game and other fun. I told him about Camp GLP, and he's going to go, too! Once I made an effort to pull myself up, the Universe supported me in awe-inspiring ways. I know I can count on that.

There may have been times in your life where there was nothing specific to look forward to. Most likely you felt a need at those times to create something to anticipate with joy. My "thing" is travel. Yours may be events closer to home, family happenings such as weddings or births, or even the completion of a project. Whatever it is, it serves as a beacon of hope, and a reason to hang tough in the rough times.

"Let yourself be silently drawn by the strange pull of what you really love. It will not lead you astray." Anonymous

To Ponder: What am I looking forward to? If nothing comes to mind quickly, create something. How does it feel in my body to have something fun to anticipate?

Ponderings

Question Everything (O)

In a culture where perfectionism reigns, and along with it the need to be a know-it-all, not nearly enough questioning occurs. We assume way too much.

Here's what happens. In an effort to appear as though we do have all the answers, we don't ask questions, and those we interact with assume we do know it all. Therefore, they don't offer us valuable information which, in fact, we don't know. We lose out, and it's a double-whammy when our assumed knowledge is incorrect.

Our independent-minded culture makes us quite averse to asking for help. While many believe asking for help is a sign of weakness, it is just the opposite. It's a sign of strength, of willingness to learn and an openness to new possibilities.

Another area where questioning has acquired a bad rap is religion. Believers are given a set of dogma and told "thou shalt not question." Some are even made to believe that questioning is a sin. That thought alone makes <u>me</u> want to question!

Here's another aspect of a know-it-all attitude: pretending to know when we don't is actually lying. It's falsehood. It's hiding yourself. Dang, what an unpleasant thought!

It is an enormous relief when one releases the need to appear to know it all. It's just another false mask we adopt and present to the world, and it is impossible to sustain. Dropping the mask and developing a questioning approach to life actually brings us way more knowledge and wisdom than a know-it-all attitude ever could.

"It ain't what you don't know that gets you into trouble. It's what you know for sure that just ain't so." Mark Twain

To Ponder: Wonder about everything. Adopt a child-like curiosity. Ask questions. What did I learn? What else am I curious about? What next step can I take to pursue my curiosity?

Ponderings

Salvation (W)

Given the religious climate of our day, I am periodically asked if I have been saved. I am usually so stunned by this question asked by someone who barely knows me that I don't have a good, quick answer. Saved from <u>what</u>? I am guessing the answer would be some sort of eternal damnation.

Common belief in most every religion is that the supreme intelligence, whatever one chooses to name it, is omnipotent, omniscient and omnipresent. For ease of discussion, I'll use "Life" as my generic term for the supreme intelligence. Another common belief is that there is an aspect of us, which I will refer to as "soul," which is eternal and exists beyond the space and time limits of our earthly bodies.

Omnipresent means that there is nowhere that Life is not evident. All things visible and invisible are manifestations of this Life. Even the apparent emptiness of space is necessary for the proper working of the galaxies. There is nowhere we could go that would be outside of Life because it is everywhere.

Omniscient means that the consciousness of Life is aware and knowing everywhere. We can't pull one over on it—we live and move and have our beings in it. It is this all-knowingness, this all-pervading consciousness, that makes all of life work in perfect, divine order, from our tiniest cells to the greatest galaxies.

Omnipotent means that Life is all-powerful, 100%. If it is everywhere, and it knows everything, it follows easily that there can be no power in opposition to it. (This leaves no room for a devil.) It is all good, or it would have self-destructed.

This Life from which our souls come forth endows us with free will. Making the transition into earthly form enables us to experience Life in myriad new ways of our choosing. Life doesn't force or restrain us from doing or experiencing anything. We choose. Therefore, my contention is that if any sort of salvation is needed, it would be to save us from our own self-damaging behaviors, and only we ourselves can do that. We may choose to use one of the great Masters, such as Jesus, as a role model, and make changes in ourselves to live as he did, but our selected Master doesn't save us, we do.

"Work out your own salvation. Do not depend on others." Buddha

To Ponder: What are my beliefs relative to salvation? Am I depending on something outside myself to save me or "fix" me?

Ponderings

You Are Not a Sinner (W)

Whether or not you participate in an organized religion, you've probably been exposed to the idea that humans are sinners, innately flawed, and only some outside force (such as Jesus) can save us from ourselves. Let me be blunt… that's bullshit, and it has been used for centuries to manipulate and repress people.

Every one of us is an emanation of pure spirit, a part of universal life energy having an adventure here on Playground Earth. It's time to stop thinking of yourself as flawed in any way. Sure, we all do dumb stuff, stuff that does not support our well-being, but that's just part of living, not a statement of unworthiness. Seeing oneself and everyone else as sinners makes for an ugly mentality towards life, always striving to measure up to some impossible (and non-existent) standard. It's living in a constant state of "I'm not good enough." That crushes the spirit within us.

You are good enough, always have been, always will be, and I'm talking eternity, not just this lifetime. Your life experience becomes vastly different and quite glorious once you begin to value yourself as the awesome creation that you are. You open your heart without fear, allowing love and joy to circulate through and around you. You recognize your dreams and aspirations and pursue them. You allow your innate creativity to flow. You see others as you see yourself, all valuable pieces in the great puzzle of life. You live and let live.

This all comes from within you, thank goodness, no need to wait for a savior to come along. It's a conscious choice to return to the knowing of the spirit from whence you came. The freedom of understanding who you are is a power and a pleasure beyond comparison.

"When you get to a place where you understand that love and belonging, your worthiness, is a birthright and not something you have to earn, anything is possible." Brene Brown

To Ponder: Do I see myself as a sinner? Where did that belief come from? Is it serving me? If I see myself as a valuable, vital and necessary part of life, how does that feel? How can I live with that as my fundamental belief about myself?

Ponderings

Have To or Get To (A)

Here's an attitude check for how you go about your life. Start by observing your thoughts or speech relative to a task in front of you. Which set of words do you use? Chances are good that if it truly is a required task, the words are "have to." I have to do the laundry. I have to buy groceries. I have to run errands. I have to pick up the kids. Seeing all these daily "have to" statements together gives the feel of drudgery to life, that it's just an endless line of inescapable tasks, then you die. That's no fun.

How about changing "have to" to "get to"? For a bit of background, I was laid up long ago for six weeks while a painful back injury healed. When I was finally able to move around comfortably enough to return to normal household tasks, I was thrilled to "get to" do the laundry, to be well enough to do that mundane chore.

We switch one word, and the entire feel of life changes. I get to buy groceries. I get to run errands. I get to pick up my kids. I'll bet you can feel from these statements that there is now a huge element of gratitude inherent in these statements. I have the means to buy groceries. I have transportation to run errands. I have kids to collect. "Get to" feels so much better. It brings an element of joy and contentment into our everyday tasks. What a difference one tiny word can make!

"Life's up and downs provide windows of opportunity to determine your values and goals. Think of using all obstacles as stepping stones to build the life you want." Marsha Sinetar

To Ponder: What do I have to do today? What happens if I approach those tasks with a "get to" attitude? How can I incorporate gratitude into the mundane chores? How does this change of focus feel?

Ponderings

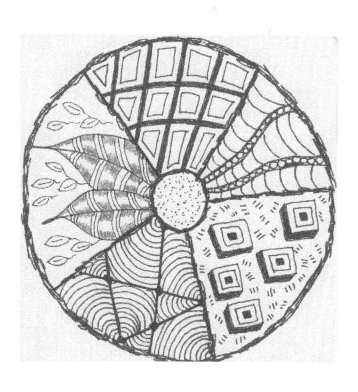

Bucket List (A)

For many years I've had three overarching goals in life. The first is to work only for God, that is, to be self-employed. The second is to never wear panty hose again. The third is to live long enough to see the Cubs win the World Series. I am self-employed, though I do work for an accountant for three months of the year doing taxes, to support my travel habit. It's a very acceptable compromise on my first goal. I'm 100% on the second one so far. The Cubs took care of the third one for me in 2016.

I do have a written bucket list that I add items to and check off when completed. It's valuable to me to have it in writing so that I don't forget or let things drift off into the mindless "someday." If it makes my bucket list, it really is important to me.

You don't have to be old or terminally ill to create a bucket list. It doesn't have to be cast in concrete either. Items can come and go as we move through life and priorities change.

One of my bucket list items is to see a game in every Major League Baseball stadium. I made a list of all the ones I've been to so far, nine, and thought, "OK, I'll get to at least one a year." Then I realized, "I'm 60, and have 21 to go, better amp it up to more than one a year!" It has been great fun to consider how to plan my travels to go to the various stadiums.

We live on a magnificent planet with astounding variety and amazing human beings. Start planning now how you want to experience it all. It's never too early or too late to make a bucket list.

"Tell me, what is it you plan to do with your one wild and precious life." Mary Oliver

To Ponder: Below is my bucket list. What would I love to do? What steps can I take to check off the most important item? Keep going from there, adding and checking off. Have fun!

Ponderings

Affirmations (A)

The hush of Heaven holds my heart today. This is an affirmation from a lesson in "A Course in Miracles." Doesn't that feel good? It makes my heart peaceful and happy.

There's loads of talk about affirmations, and no doubt zillions of Google search results. The ironic thing is that we are using them all the time, even if it is unconscious. We're always talking to ourselves mentally, and most of it is repetitive. Even if it's negative, if we are saying it over and over to ourselves, it's an affirmation.

Some folks use affirmations to create a desired result. That is an excellent use, as it keeps us focused on a desired outcome. Lots of things can get in our way when we set out to achieve a goal, and affirmations help us navigate a cluttered path and stay tuned into the result. From early on in the writing of this book, I had a clear picture of what the final product would look like. I held that picture in my thoughts as my affirmation of its creation, along with the simple thought, "It's gonna happen."

I like to use affirmations as a means to control my thinking. There is an extraordinary amount of negativity surrounding each of us, and it is so easy to get mentally sucked into it. The challenge is to reach for a better-feeling thought. I recently experienced a minor but lengthy illness, and I don't do "sick" well. I kept mentally tugging myself back to a favorite affirmation: Everything within my cellular structure is changeable, because each molecule is a piece of God. I am whole, I am healthy and I am holy.

One essential aspect of an effective affirmation is that you believe it to be true or possible. If you don't, no amount of repetition will make it work for you. Make sure the affirmation feels good to you. It doesn't have to be a literary work of art either. Simple works. That's why "Life is good" is so popular. That's a super affirmation, by the way.

I'd suggest, too, that you keep your affirmations to yourself. What you tell yourself is of no concern to anyone else. The desires of your heart matter to you, so use that heartfelt power to affirm a joyful life for yourself.

"The most rewarding thing for me has been this affirmation that people are basically good and smart, and if you give them a simple tool that allows them to exhibit that behavior, they'll prove it to you every single day." Biz Stone

To Ponder: Below is an affirmation that expresses my heartfelt desire. How does it feel in my body? Repeat it frequently. Note subsequent results from the use of this affirmation.

Ponderings

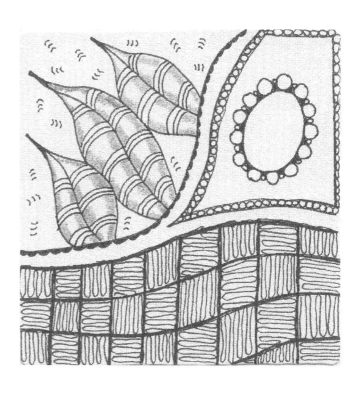

Road Trip (A)

These words are joyous music to my ears. I love to travel, go, see and do. I also love to organize road trips, yes, I do.

First of all, there's the day trip. I have a friend, Phil, who along with me, is dedicated to exploring our home state of Kansas and to eating homemade pie. We make it a point to visit a site of interest, and then to zero in on a great local restaurant for lunch. There's always room for pie. We have a whole day to talk, and we cover everything. It's a "slice of heaven" in so many ways.

Then there's the weekend trip, an overnighter or two for an event such as a workshop or concert or retreat. My favorite way to do this is to send an email to a bunch of friends which describes the event, and say, "The first three folks who say 'me, me!' get to go with me." Others can go, too, it's just that I can only fit three others in my car.

On a grander scale, every couple of years I take a several-thousand-mile driving trip for some event, usually "back east," that includes lots of family visits. I also use these trips to fulfill my bucket list item of seeing a game in every MLB ballpark. While I don't necessarily love to drive, it's great to get out of my routine for a couple weeks and have so much alone time. I love the adventure, and I really love coming home.

The pinnacle of road trips is international travel. My good friend, Lanie, and I have committed to doing an international trip every even-numbered year. So far we've done Mexico, Italy and Scotland/Ireland. We are both blessed with husbands who don't want to go, and who encourage us to go. Bonus! We approach every trip with this question: if this is the last trip we take together, where do we most want to go? I do, on these international trips, leave the organization to a tour company. Lanie and I agree that on trips overseas, we want to be pampered, and we are fine being tourists in a group.

Wanna have some fun? Wanna get away? Use these ideas and create an adventure of your own. Here's a secret: folks love going on road trips when someone else organizes them. Here's another secret: you do have time for a road trip.

"Blessed are the curious, for they shall have adventures." Lovelle Drachman

To Ponder: Where would I like to go? Organize a road trip. Describe the adventure. How did it feel to get away for a while? What's my next adventure?

Ponderings

Baby Steps (A)

There's great wisdom in the old, old saying: Rome wasn't built in a day. Nor was a book written, or a business built, or a masterpiece composed or a degree completed. If someone is even brave enough to consider being inspired to create, it's so easy to get discouraged by the seeming monstrosity of the project, especially if there is a learning curve involved, too, which is usually the case.

"Ya gotta start somewhere." The Universe is literally overflowing with ideas. We've all had them. Some we use, some find other homes. Those that stir your heartstrings, that won't leave you alone, that really excite you, those are the ones to pursue. You don't need to know everything at the start. It's like following a trail of crumbs. Just getting started with one baby step leads to the next step and the next, and with diligence, to the masterpiece. Having experienced this process, the end result is quite awesome, but it is the process of baby-stepping that's truly the reward for one's efforts. A creative life is a joyful life.

Another area of life where a baby step is a critical mindset is in improving one's health. Big changes all at once ("I'm going to lose 25 pounds and completely revamp my diet") are self-defeating and nearly always unsustainable. How about just walking around the block in the sunshine once a day? How about not buying the weekly bag of Fritos? Research is showing that when we make baby step changes such as these, they are much more likely to lead to lasting improvement. The baby step change makes us feel better, inspiring us to look for more baby step changes, and so it goes, fairly painless, permanent health improvements.

"Starting something is the best way to finish something. And just doing a teeny, tiny something today, anything, from wherever you are, is the best way to start something."
Mike Dooley

To Ponder: What creation would I like to bring into the world? What baby step can I take to get started? Is there some way in which I'd like to improve my health? What small habit can I incorporate into my day?

Ponderings

Heaven (W)

Do you ever give a thought to heaven? I'm not talking about afterlife here, the place we supposedly get to go if we are "good enough." That's not a part of my belief system, nor is the idea of hell.

You may have heard the phrase "kingdom of heaven" but I prefer "queendom of heaven." Heaven is not the serious, judgment-laden, competition-to-get-in concept that religions have made it out to be. Heaven is simply the choice to live a joyful, full, rich, loving life right now. That's what Jesus meant when he said, "The kingdom of heaven is at hand." It's right here, right now, for the choosing. (Note that men wrote the Bible, so "queendom" would never have been considered.) If we choose to disregard the good that is continually present in our lives, soon life does become quite hellish.

You may have used the phrase "this is heaven!" to describe a particularly wonderful food, vacation, garment or event. Your statement is the truth. Heaven is finding utter joy in the moment. When we practice finding good in each moment, those moments string together into the heavenly life I described above.

Don't reserve "heaven!" for just the "big" things in life. See it in your child's smile, a neighbor's wave, a rosebud, sunshine, music, laughter, colors, a thunderstorm, and snowflakes. The more we practice seeing things as heavenly, the more heavenly things come into our lives. It's spiritual principle.

Who knows what happens when we pass from earthly life? Given that we're already in heaven, I'm guessing it's just more and greater heaven.

"My soul can find no staircase to Heaven unless it be through Earth's loveliness."
Michelangelo

To Ponder: What are my beliefs relative to heaven? Are they serving me? How can I incorporate more heaven into my life here and now?

Ponderings

They Don't Care (W)

We spend a ridiculously enormous amount of time wondering and worrying about what other people think of us. I'm going to let you in on a little secret: they don't care!!!!!

What? There is an infinite amount of judgment, criticism, advice, gossip and opinion being spewed everywhere you turn. It's all mindless chatter to keep the focus on you instead of the spewer. That way the spewer gets a respite from dealing with his own issues. Therefore, he is simply using you for personal gain. See? It's all about them, they don't care about you.

Look at your own life. You are busy. You have enough work, home life, activities, family, extended family and health considerations to keep you occupied for way more than 24 hours a day. If you are taking good care of yourself and successfully managing your own life, you have little time to spend concentrating on someone else's issues.

I'm not saying you should not be supportive or helpful towards others. Be a good friend. One way to do that is to instill confidence in others that they can resolve their own issues. You really don't want others meddling in your life, so don't do it to them. Each of us lives in the world he or she has created, and no one else can know all the details. It's easier to stay out of another's business. Since we are all immersed in our own little universe, we're quite busy with its upkeep and don't really care about anyone else's universe.

If we all take care of our own universe and make it a happy place for us to be, there's no need to spy into another's world.

"Nobody came here to be the keeper of you, and you did not come here to be the keeper of anybody else." Abraham-Hicks

To Ponder: Is someone meddling in my universe? Why are they really doing that? Is it really a concern for me? Am I spying into another's world, offering advice or criticism? If so, why am I doing that? Is it helpful? Do I really care?

Ponderings

"I Love My Life" (W)

I was on a group phone call recently with friends, and this phrase was brought up as a topic of conversation. Specifically, the question was raised whether we could state it and truly mean it. I have been saying "I love my life" with great conviction for years. I use that phrase pretty much every morning in my prayers. Saying I love my life simply brings me more to love.

What does it mean to me to love my life? It certainly doesn't mean everything is swimmingly perfect all the time. In general I am mostly joyful, but I do experience the full range of emotions, and I am grateful for that. I have wonderful people in my life who are loving and supportive. My life is abundant to the fullest extent of that term, not just speaking of money. I love baseball! I love the varied work I do, and I especially love the freedom and flexibility I have to travel. I get to teach and practice yoga and expand my spiritual nature. I enjoy being on Playground Earth at this time. I am creative and have useful talents. I am comfortable in my own skin.

But then there's house-cleaning, laundry, inattentive drivers, cancelled flights, flat tires, colds and viruses, poor customer service, broken appliances... myriad potential annoyances. They, too, are a part of the life I love, because I'm grateful that I have the strength, resiliency and resources to deal with them.

I believe we choose to come into this life. Why not love it?

"I have found that if you love life, life will love you back." Arthur Rubinstein

To Ponder: Can I say I love my life and truly mean it? Why or why not? If not, what would it take for me to love my life?

Ponderings

Doing Nothing (A)

A Spanish proverb states: How beautiful it is to do nothing, and then rest afterward.

I am a dedicated napper, so much so that I consider napping to be one of my hobbies. When I ran across this proverb, I thought, "That's me!" Yet as I pondered this saying further, I realized that I'm not so clear about doing nothing, just the rest afterward part.

We live in a time and culture when accomplishment is the almighty grail. To do nothing is lazy, wasting time, even somewhat socially unacceptable. We hardly even celebrate those almighty accomplishments in our pursuit of busy-ness.

What is "doing nothing" anyway? Is it meditating? Is it reading? Is it laying around watching sports (one of my favorite activities)? Is it sitting in the park and watching the world go by? Is it watching paint dry or grass grow? Is it chatting with someone you love over a beer or a cup of coffee? Is napping "doing nothing"? How about leisurely blogging? Is it lying in the sun on a tropical beach?

It seems that "doing nothing" is a very personal thing. I would add that it is an essential part of life, otherwise life just becomes one endless rat race. Here you go: you officially have my permission to spend some time doing nothing.

"Taking time to do nothing often brings everything into perspective." Doe Zantamata

To Ponder: What do I consider "doing nothing," and how can I incorporate more of it into my life? Does "doing nothing" make me uncomfortable? If so, explore those feelings further.

Ponderings

Best Day Yet (O)

This heading comes from a story by David Goldberg, wherein a friend of his family, when asked how he was doing, consistently said, "Best day yet!" Mr. Goldberg indicated that this friend is in his 90s. That phrase struck a very harmonious chord with me. I use it often and share it with friends and students.

One result of a "best day yet!" attitude is that even if a day is fairly ordinary, including such basic human tasks as grocery shopping and laundry, I have a greater appreciation of being able to do those ordinary things.

This simple phrase enhances my awareness that as life continues to get better and better for me, every additional day on Planet Earth is a huge blessing. Granted, my life has its down times, too, and, eventually, I am grateful to be here to experience even those.

There's also a creative aspect to the "best day yet!" mentality. Reminding myself upon waking that the Universe is conspiring with me to make this day truly my best ever, the act of anticipating good in my life makes it much more likely to appear. I love surprises, and it's so thrilling when a day includes some extra-bonus goodness.

It's a matter of focus. "Best day yet!" lets us focus on the uplifting, joyful, bountiful good in our lives, rather than the negativity of people and situations surrounding us. Say "best day yet!" like you mean it, and see how good it feels.

"If you don't think every day is a good day, just try missing one." Cavett Robert

To Ponder: How can I work the "best day yet!" idea into my day? How did it change my day?

Ponderings

Make Some Art (A)

I don't feel in any way talented when it comes to art using a brush, i.e. painting. I can draw a mean stick figure or paint the walls in my house, and that's about it. With some trepidation and great curiosity, I recently went with friends to a group picture-painting experience. Everyone has their own canvas and paints, and a very patient instructor leads the group through the process of painting a chosen picture. Our group did flowers. I loved the whole experience.

Make some art. There are myriad forms to choose from such as music, painting, fabric art, gardening, cooking, baking, coloring, photography, stained glass, collage, dancing, drawing or flower-arranging. Even if you don't think you are good at anything, make some art anyway. Here's why:

- It gets your creative juices flowing. This may not happen routinely, and this benefits your entire life.
- Breaking your routine and making some art is a centering act that is both calming and energizing.
- It helps you develop your intuition as you explore within to see what your heart wants to create.
- You learn something, both about the art form and yourself.
- You learn self-acceptance. Your art truly matters only to you, and so what if it's not "perfect" or others don't approve. You learn to stand firmly and joyfully with what you've created.
- You get to practice releasing judgment of yourself (and others). Let it go. Keep on creating.
- You don't know what you can do until you give it a try.
- It's fun.

I experienced all of these things creating my flower picture. It makes me want to go make some more art.

"The purpose of art is washing the dust of daily life off our souls." Pablo Picasso

To Ponder: What kind of creating sounds like fun to me? Do it. What did I experience in the process? Make more art.

Ponderings

Your Vibration (H)

I have attempted through these short writings to challenge your mind and stretch your considerations of how things are. Maybe that's happened a little, maybe a lot. Here's another challenge—your body is energy. Not <u>has</u> energy, <u>is</u> energy. That energy moves at a particular vibratory level, and as you move through your day, you are continually adjusting your vibration.

There are lots of ways in which "the body is energy" shows up in life. Starting first with your own body, notice the warmth, your heart beating, the gentle tingling of your very busy cells doing what they do. You feel energized after a good night's sleep, with high vibration. You feel a low-energy vibration after a long, hard day.

We have all experienced walking into a group setting and being aware of a very high, joyful, fun vibration or a low, tense, uncomfortable one. That's the combination of the energy vibrations of the people there. Positive emotions of love, joy, gratitude and peace are higher on the vibratory scale than the so-called negative emotions such as fear, anger, hate and resentment.

Another example of the body's vibration is the "energy vampire." That is a person who seems to suck out all your energy when you spend time around them. Often you can't really "put your finger on" what causes this, but you know being around that person leaves you exhausted.

Have you ever felt sore the next day after you tried a new form of exercise? That is energy moving in your body in places where it was not moving before. Despite how it may feel, that is a good thing. Keep exercising to keep those energy pathways open. It is when those energy pathways get clogged that we develop aches and pains, and over the long-term, chronic conditions such as arthritis.

Your ability to affect your personal vibration is of utmost importance. Your vibration attracts others with a similar vibratory level. Therefore you can select via your vibration what and whom you attract into your life. Hanging at a low vibration attracts negativity into your life. Hanging at an energized, loving vibration attracts love into your experience. Your high vibration has the power to lift others' vibrations, enabling you to be a mighty force for good in the world.

"Celebration carries a high vibration of joy, and joy is mixed with a great dose of gratitude, and gratitude is a creative energy that creates more gratitude." Eugene Holden

To Ponder: Close my eyes, sit calmly and observe my body energy. How does my vibration feel now? Moving through the day, observe the connection between my energy level and what is happening around me. What did I notice? What people or activities support a high vibration in me? How can I incorporate more of them into my life?

Ponderings

The World in Which You Live (W)

By this point, if you've hung in here, examining your life and considering different belief possibilities, you may be wondering if anything has actually changed in you. This is an excellent time to ask that question of someone close to you, as others see changes in us much more quickly than we see them.

You didn't become your current self overnight. It has been a lifelong process with myriad people and experiences to bring you to where you are, like it or not. All growth happens in consciousness first. We learn to change our thinking, and then our outer experience changes to match that expanding consciousness.

Ponder the idea that each human is creating their own movie, "This Is My Life." Each person is the director of his or her own show, with complete control over the characters, plot, action, dialogue and scenery. Thought is the guiding power. We can let that power run amok, or we can take control and use it to our advantage. An analogy would be sailing a sailboat. We can let the wind simply blow it around and not get anywhere, or we can take hold of the rudder and use the wind to take us to our destination.

It is a powerful shift to take responsibility for creating the world in which you live, all of it, good or bad. We are all, at best, fledglings in handling this responsibility. We create messes. We blame others. We wonder why things happen. We let others meddle in our movies to our detriment. All of this creates a mighty opportunity for compassion towards ourselves and others. We're all in that same sailboat.

One way to start taking charge of your own movie is to notice when something in another person bothers you. Whatever that something is, it's a reflection of the same thing in yourself that bugs you. We project it onto someone else to avoid looking at it in ourselves. One example from my life is frustration with poor driving skills. As soon as I fuss to myself about someone else's driving, I find myself not paying attention and doing something sloppy. Another example… as a yoga teacher and spiritual living coach, I often feel discouraged at other's unwillingness to do even simple things that would improve their well-being. Uh, look at my own life, there's loads of opportunity for improvement there if I'd only get busy on it!

You have way more power to affect the world in which you live than you knew. So does everyone else. Each one who harnesses that power creates a better world for all.

"Perception is a mirror, not a fact. And what I look on is my state of mind, reflected outward." A Course in Miracles

To Ponder: What is changing in me and my world? What isn't changing that I would like to change? What reflections of myself do I see in others?

Ponderings

Alone Time (H)

Feelings are mixed relative to spending time alone. Some folks passionately avoid it, others can't live without it, and there's lots of other points between. It's a personal choice. While there is no right or wrong concerning alone time, there are some advantages to regularly having it.

Alone time enables you to "recharge your batteries." It gives you time to think without distraction, explore your life, and consider your choices. It can be a mighty head-clearing experience. It can also enhance your self-sufficiency, by making you able to care for and entertain yourself, make your own decisions, and resolve your own problems. It is an even greater recharge if you can unplug from your electronic devices and truly disconnect.

Time alone sparks creativity. First of all, you decide what to do during your "me" time, and it can involve all sorts of creative activities, such as making art, exploring a new place or learning a new skill. Using your creativity is energizing, another bonus of alone time.

Relationships can be greatly enhanced when both parties take time for themselves. It promotes a feeling of independence rather than clinging and neediness. Caring for oneself using alone time means there is more to give to the relationship.

If alone time is new to you, start small. Pick one activity you enjoy, schedule it and do it. Make it a regular habit. Alone time is not selfish—ignore those voices in your head or elsewhere that would tell you it is. You live with yourself 24/7. You may as well enjoy the company.

"You only grow when you are alone." Paul Newman

To Ponder: Plan alone time for myself. What do I want to do? Do it. How did it go? How did it feel to have that time alone? What will my next solo adventure be?

Ponderings

What's Wrong? What's Right? (W/O/A)

This writing is inspired by the movie, I AM, by Tom Shadyak. He begins with the question, "What's wrong with the world?" He ends up with the question, "What's right with the world?"

This is another invitation to pay attention to your own thoughts and feelings. Note how you feel when you say or think, "what's wrong with ...?" For instance, "what's wrong with me?" Is there anything about that self-judgmental statement that feels good? I believe most of us have at least thought, "what's wrong with you?!?!?" relative to someone we love. I feel anger and frustration in that, not a pleasant or productive way to interact.

On the other hand, "what's right with ...?" leads your thinking or conversation in a whole different direction. It feels uplifting. It feels hopeful. It's encouraging. The potential is much greater for good to come from it.

Imagine if each of us started viewing our lives and our immediate surroundings and those we come in contact with from the standpoint of "what's right with ... ?" Every single moment and interaction is more enjoyable. Life becomes a simple state of contentment rather than a problem to be fixed. We operate from our strengths rather than our weaknesses.

What's right with the world? You are!

"Take up one idea. Make that one idea your life—think of it, dream of it, live on that idea. Let the brain, muscles, nerves, every part of your body, be full of that idea. This is the way to success." Swami Vivekananda

To Ponder: Notice my tendency to focus on the wrongs in my life. Turn those around to rights. How does this practice feel and affect me?

Ponderings

Don't Take Anything Personally (O)

This is another of "The Four Agreements" from the book by that name by Don Miguel Ruiz. This agreement is quite challenging because as humans, we generally believe the world revolves around us, and "it's ALL about me." This is what Mr. Ruiz calls "personal importance," the maximum expression of selfishness.

Whatever other people do or say is completely about them, not about you. Always and forever, amen! They are operating from their life experience and behaving based on that. It has nothing to do with you. (See **They Don't Care**, p. 186.) Their actions are a result of their internal belief system, and particularly a reflection of how they value themselves. If you are susceptible to others' opinions, you make yourself vulnerable to poisoning your own life. Taking things personally means you choose to suffer.

If someone says or does something that hurts you, it is because it has touched a wound or issue within you, and you choose to be hurt by it. Rather than lashing out at the person whom you believe hurt you, this is an opportunity to look within and heal the wound. That way, you don't take personally similar incidents in the future. Hurtful behaviors tend to repeat until we heal the wounds.

Taking things personally is an indicator that you are living in fear. There's the fear of ridicule or rejection, the fear that the negative things said about you may be true. You are on constant alert to protect and defend yourself from others. That's no way to live.

Don't take anything personally applies equally to praise. Same thing, it's about them, not you. If you live from a place of already knowing you are wonderful and worthy, there's no need for praise.

"If you keep this agreement, you can travel around the world with your heart completely wide open and no one can hurt you." Don Miguel Ruiz

To Ponder: Describe my most recent incident of taking something personally. How did I feel? What if I didn't take it personally? How can I practice this agreement in my life?

Ponderings

None of Your Business (A)

Recently I was labeled a "hypocrite" by a close relative applying this term to a group in which I was participating. I believe it was not directed at me specifically. There was no hypocrisy as charged personally in my participation. Alas, there was a woeful failure to check facts before the nasty label was applied. I practice very diligently at living in integrity, so this accusation stung a bit.

One very wise old saying is useful here: "It takes one to know one." If we are judging someone and labeling them as "bad" in some way, it's because we are well-acquainted with that behavior. We wouldn't recognize or judge them if that tendency was not active within us.

Another very wise old saying is: "When you point the finger, three fingers are pointing back at you." Same deal, if you see it in someone else, especially if you feel called to bring her attention to it, it would be wise to look for that same behavior in your own life.

I can't reinforce enough that other folks' actions and manner of living are none of your business. From the outside looking in, you have no clue what is truly going on in another's life. You have absolutely no basis to judge or criticize another. In the personal instance described above, were I not practicing "don't take anything personally," this judgmental labeling could have caused considerable harm in an otherwise close relationship. There was truly no need to even express such a comment.

Judgment begets judgment. I offer that it's extremely likely that the more you stay out of others' business, the more they will stay out of yours. It's a win-win for all.

"I don't get how people get so anti-something. Mind your own business, take care of your own affairs, and don't worry about other people so much." Betty White

"If you mind your own business, you'll stay busy all the time." Hank Williams Jr.

To Ponder: In what ways am I judging others? Do I feel the need to comment? How is that working for me? Where do I see in my own life these behaviors that I am judging?

Ponderings

A Good Day to Die (W)

Here's a hot topic, one's own death. This may range from uncomfortable to pure terror, and it's definitely not a hot topic—we'd prefer to deny it out of existence. However, you can greatly enhance how you live your days by considering the end of them.

Time flies, and as a sixty-something, I can verify that it flies faster the older I become. As you age, the pace of friends, family and acquaintances passing greatly accelerates. Each transition encourages me to ponder whether I'm living my life to my greatest satisfaction.

The phrase "Today is a good day to die" is attributed to Crazy Horse. What does that mean to us in our daily living? If you passed today, would you leave with your life in fairly good order? I don't mean the house clean and checkbook balanced. Are your relationships good? Have you told those you love that you do love and appreciate them? Have you made amends and mended any broken relationships? Do you have any regrets about what you haven't or have done? Do you get to enjoy at least some part of each day, and contribute to the world in a satisfying way? After you pass, are folks going to say the things about you that you would want them to say? Have you made good progress checking off a personal bucket list?

I think it would be glorious to pass away quickly and quietly while sunning on a magnificent tropical beach somewhere. However, that would require me to hang out on a beach for an unknown number of years. That isn't practical. A more likely way to go along these lines would be for me to pass while golfing or swimming at the local YMCA. I have an annual three-month full-time job preparing tax returns. Would I like to pass while doing that? That's not a great thought, but at least I'd be providing a useful service and doing work I enjoy and for which I am well-suited.

Examining what makes today a good day to die will give you great perspective on what is truly important to you. That's very valuable knowledge.

"When I was young, I wanted to live fast and die young. Now that I'm old, I want to live young and die fast." Author Unknown

To Ponder: Is today a good day for me to die? Elaborate. Are there some things I would like to resolve, do or finish? What is holding me back?

Ponderings

Those "Annoying" Bodily Functions (H)

My life as a yoga teacher and practitioner is dedicated to helping fellow students get intimately in touch with their bodies. This is a great practice whether or not you do yoga. Our bodies are fascinating mysteries, even with our ever-expanding scientific knowledge.

Let's for the sake of space just consider three annoying bodily functions: farting, burping and crying. Most folks don't like doing any of these in public. My mother once told me that no self-respecting woman would ever burp or fart in public. She died early, at age 61. Connection?

These annoying bodily functions are supremely important to our overall wellbeing. If we didn't need these capabilities, we would not have them. Go ahead, admit it, you enjoy the relief of a good fart. You even smile!

Anyone who has been around or raised children knows that farts are one of the great delights of childhood. We raised two sons, so we even had a practice of rating them on a scale of 1-10. I tell all my new yoga students that it's OK to fart and OK to laugh about it. Instead of being embarrassed by farting, why not bring back some of that childhood enjoyment? My husband educated me early on in our marriage about the college-student entertainment of fart lighting (no details here!). There are apps that offer different farting sounds. Anyone who has ever slept with another person has most likely experienced the "Dutch Oven." That's when one person holds down the covers, then farts, then fluffs the covers. Eww, gross! But "made you laugh!"

Another essential relief talent we possess is burping. If you've ever tried to prevent a burp, you know how important this function is. Notice your pets—they do it with abandon, and don't feel anything but relief. That's a good lesson right there. My husband taught our sons to say a word or phrase when they burp. I've never been that coordinated.

Lastly, we turn to crying. I've seen folks actually mortified when crying in a group setting. It seems that some public places are OK for crying, such as funerals, and some places are definitely not OK, such as a work setting. What is it about not crying? Are we trying to prove that our lives are so perfect that we never cry? Maybe we were discouraged from crying as children, a great disservice, but not a belief we need to retain. I refer to crying as soul-rinsing, which must happen periodically to keep our souls fresh and open.

The point of all this is to lighten up and appreciate your body for all it can do. Everybody farts, burps and cries. Therefore, you are not less of a human being if you do so.

"I tell you, we are here on Earth to fart around, and don't let anybody tell you different."
Kurt Vonnegut

"My philosophy of dating is to just fart right away." Jenny McCarthy

To Ponder: Am I uptight about farting, burping or crying? Why? How might I lighten up my attitude toward these "annoying" bodily functions?

Ponderings

Drama (H)

There's WAY TOO MUCH of it! (That was drama in writing, get it!?!?)

I am writing this at the beginning of the Trump Presidency, and drama pretty well sums up the entire proceedings, all sides, all the time. It's exhausting, sucking up an extraordinary amount of energy for no good purpose. Drama has infiltrated the press and has created the discouraging situation wherein we can't rely on many news sources to deliver "just the facts, ma'am."

You probably don't have to look very far in your own life or someone else's to see that drama is addictive. If some is good, more is better. People vie for who can create the most drama. The importance of one's life seems to be based on how much drama swirls around them. Drama sells "news" and products. It can be temporarily energizing.

Like all addictions, there is a downside. Drama is often intimately tied with gossip, an exceedingly nasty habit. We have to create or consume ever greater amounts of drama to sustain the "high." The need for more always increases, it never decreases. It encourages the self-defeating habit of comparing yourself to others, to see whose life has the most drama. Drama regularly leads to misunderstandings, which can damage relationships. Drama creates "mountains out of molehills," and who needs that?

Drama is unnecessary. We can leave it to the theater and movies, enjoy it there, leave it there, and go home in peace.

"Drama's not safe and it's not pretty and it's not kind." Russell T. Davies

To Ponder: Where is there drama in my life? Do I get a high from it? What would it take to let it go?

Ponderings

The Right to Say Yes or No (A)

Everyone has the right to say yes or no. That includes you. Much as we like to think we are the special exception to the rule, on this one, there are no exceptions. You have the right to say yes or no.

Wow. Really?!?!? I can say "no" when I mean it? Yes! It does no one, especially you, any good when you say "yes" when you really want to say "no." Doing that puts you in a position where you really do not want to be, and that leads to all sorts of resentments and emotional complications, not to mention pouring time and energy into something to which you are not committed. It's ugly for all concerned.

The same applies to the situation where you say "no" when you really want to say "yes." You really want to do something that ignites your spirit, but "should" or "shouldn't" enters the picture and you decline. This, too, leads to resentments and emotional complications, and missing out on (yet another) heart's desire. It's ugly for all concerned.

One other item about this particular right: you do not need to justify your answer in any way. That means you do not need to apologize for it, even if it is not to the recipient's liking. You don't need to explain your choice. Simply state it with confidence. Saying what you mean is another ongoing life practice that gets easier the more often you follow your heart.

"A 'No' uttered from the deepest conviction is better than a 'Yes' merely uttered to please, or worse, to avoid trouble." Mahatma Gandhi

To Ponder: When have I said no when I wanted to say yes? When have I said yes and wanted to say no? How do those situations feel to me? How can I practice my right to say what I mean? What keeps me from saying it?

Ponderings

We Are Never Alone (W)

We have all felt alone at times, whether it's a temporary bout of loneliness or the feeling that we are the <u>only</u> one with a certain feeling or condition or whatever. For the longest (miserable) time, I thought I was the only one on the planet who had the whacked-out behaviors with food that I had. Then a dear friend called me one day and started describing his obsessive thoughts and actions with food. That gave me hope, and subsequently, I've had a wonderful life of recovery. My point here is that no matter how unique we may think we are, we are never alone. There is someone out there "in the same boat."

On a more cosmic scale, I believe we are never alone spiritually either. This spiritual presence surrounding us is here to support us as we live in this earthly plane. Does that sound silly or goofy or "woo-woo"? So what. Play with this. Act as if this presence is there, is on your side, listens when you speak to it, supports and loves you. If this practice doesn't "work," you haven't lost anything. If it does, you've gained an immeasurable power working on your behalf, all the time. You don't need to share your "secret," and you don't need to subscribe to any religion to use this power. Actually, you are using it already, just not consciously. I'm inviting you to use it by choice.

Best of all, you can envision this power however you choose, because it's your unique relationship with it. It can be a fairy godmother, superhero or Santa Claus. You get to decide.

"For beautiful eyes, look for the good in others; for beautiful lips, speak only words of kindness; and for poise, walk with the knowledge that you are never alone." Audrey Hepburn

To Ponder: How could I use an always-available supporting presence in my life? What would it be and do for me? How might I talk with it? Play with this and note the results.

Ponderings

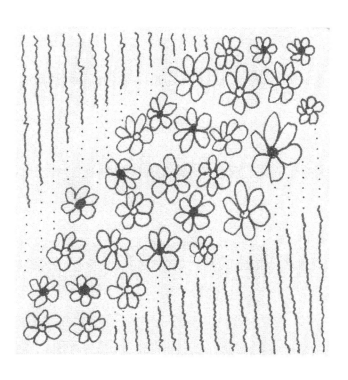

The Big Game (W/O)

Let's play "what if?" and get very imaginative. Let's say we exist in some glorious realm when we are not here in a body on Playground Earth. It's so non-stop glorious that we get bored periodically and long for adventure. So we make travel arrangements, generally outlining our earthly intentions, book transportation (i.e., a set of parents already on Earth), and arrive for our turn in the Big Game. Here's a great description written by Mike Dooley:

> When you play a game with family and friends like hide and seek, Twister, or even Monopoly, do you lose sleep the night before? Do you worry what people will think of your performance? Do you wonder how your past or your childhood years might influence your moves? Do you "replay" each turn in your mind the day after?
>
> No. Because it's just for fun. You understand that no matter what happens, nothing about it can detract from who you are. That while you might not "win," you'll be richer and wiser for the time spent thinking, and calculating, and sharing with friends. You might even relish the refinement and development of your skills. Besides, in games you have nothing to prove; everyone you play with already loves you.
>
> Bottom line, you can become more for the playing, but not less. And so, the more you play, the more fun you have, the more you grow, and the better you get.
>
> It's why you're here.
>
> The board is your life, the tokens are your friends, and achieving particular dreams and overcoming customized challenges are the prizes you've chosen ahead of time. There are health games, wealth games, and relationship games. Confidence games, pride games, and worthiness games. There are even games you've never heard of. Some play one at a time, others play many at once, but no one, ever, has anything to lose.

No one ever has anything to lose. What if...?

"Life is a song - sing it. Life is a game - play it. Life is a challenge - meet it. Life is a dream - realize it. Life is love - enjoy it." Sai Baba

To Ponder: What comes up as I consider this idea? If this idea is true, how might I live differently?

Ponderings

Your Own Authority (A)

You are a totally capable human being. Yes, you are, no matter what you may tell yourself, no matter what others may lead you to believe. You did not get to where you are today without being able to draw resources to yourself and make decisions. It's time to own up to your own authority to choose how to live your life.

One way to tap into your inner guidance or intuition is through spiritual practice. You may wonder what that is, and it may seem like some mystical practice that involves meditation for hours at a time. I have a rather non-mainstream view of spiritual practice. We are spiritual beings having a human experience (not the other way around), so <u>all</u> of life is a spiritual practice. Simple kindness in thought, word and deed, especially toward oneself, is spiritual practice. Continually affirming the support of a higher power is spiritual practice. (See **Personal Management Team**, p. 82.) Practicing yoga is, too. Being your own true self, and not whom others expect you to be, is a demanding, challenging and exciting practice. The same is true for trusting yourself.

This brings me to the subject of meditation. Nowadays, meditation is a big "should" in life that most folks think they can't do and don't have time for. Meditation teachers would have you believe that you must spend big bucks to learn to do it right, and devote hours daily to the practice. The almighty grail of meditation is to still your thoughts. Here's a secret: for the average person living an average life (i.e., not a recluse in a monastery), that ain't gonna happen, no matter how hard you try. What if meditation is simply closing the eyes, taking a few deeps breaths, choosing an item to be grateful for, and relaxing the body. How easy is that? You can do it many times a day. It feels good. It keeps you in touch with the good side of life. That's spiritual practice.

Getting to know yourself and use your intuition enables you to stand in your own authority as you move through life. It's a glorious place of comfortable power, a place where we are always practicing.

"What then is freedom? The power to live as one wishes." Marcus Tullius Cicero

To Ponder: Note ways that I am already using spiritual practice (some I may do without even thinking of them as spiritual practices—dig deep). Try the mini-meditation breaks a few times a day. Note how that feels. Do I seek others' advice before making decisions? What if I check in with my heart instead of others? Where might using my own authority lead me?

Ponderings

You Are the Answer to Someone's Prayer (W/O)

"I'm a big fat answer to someone's prayer. Only the people who "get me" should get me. They deserve my time and energy." Tama Kieves, "Inspired and Unstoppable"

I invite you to sit with this header statement for a few moments. The initial reaction may be that this isn't true for you, but I guarantee that it is, and it is not arrogant or self-centered to believe it is so. You would not be on the planet at this time if you were not filling some important role, i.e., answering someone's prayer.

You don't need to think in terms of "prayer" if that doesn't work for you. You can think of it as a call for resources or a cry for love. No doubt you've answered many of those in your life, being at just the right place at the right time to help or hug someone. How magical is that? You have been, and you are, the answer to someone's prayer. It is a natural part of living.

Another aspect of Ms. Kieves' quote above is the focusing of our life energy. Do we want to waste it on people who don't "get us," who don't approve, who don't support our choices? We'll never convince those folks, they don't deserve us. It's the folks who do see us as answered prayer, who appreciate us in all our quirky glory, that's where we want to spend our precious time and energy.

"Wherever you are, hold yourself in appreciation, commemoration, and infinite gratitude. I guarantee you there is someone who would love to be where you are." Tama Kieves

To Ponder: How have I been the answer to someone's prayer? With whom do I spend the bulk of my time? Do they "get me"? If not, how can I shift my time and energy to people who do?

Ponderings

Your Intimate Relationship with Money (A)

Like it or not, money's tendrils are intimately woven into the fabric of our lives. Fear of "not enough," the pressure to make more, wanting and not getting the things money can buy, relationship angst—the list of anxieties relative to money can go on and on. There is hope…

I devoted several months to work my way through a book titled "Emotional Currency" by Kate Levinson. The subtitle is "A Woman's Guide to Building a Healthy Relationship with Money." It is a well-written and interesting read. It is also packed with self-exploration questions. While her focus is on women and money, the questions are applicable to men also.

I investigated with writing and contemplation my history with money and the many different ways I experience money now.

I became aware of how emotionally-charged money can be for me, as well as how pervasive money-related thoughts and issues are in my life. I also discovered that I have a few money-related "unmentionables"—ideas relative to money that are quite embarrassing or even shameful that I would never speak aloud. I did share them with a trusted person, as that's how we release the shame—express it and let it go. That took some bravery on my part. The point is that we all have these "unmentionables" if we take the time to identify them.

Money is a "core" issue with me, which is ironic, as I've never not had enough. Awareness relative to our money behaviors and emotional responses to money is the first step to change. As a result to this self-exploration exercise, my angst toward money lessened significantly. Dive in, you have nothing to lose except your stress over money!

"Don't let making a living prevent you from making a life." John Wooden

To Ponder: Does spending money cause me emotional stress? Is "not enough money" always an issue? Do I have arguments with a significant other over money? Does my spending feel out of control? Do I have credit card debt? Get the book mentioned above and use it.

Ponderings

A Coach Brings Forth the Best (A)

I am a well-trained and experienced spiritual living coach. What is that and why would I care, you ask? My short explanation is: one who daily lives and expresses the compassionate consciousness of the One Life by revealing the highest and innermost Presence within herself and all life.

It's about consciousness. It is about being able to look past any apparent situation to see the truth. For instance, we may believe we are too old, too poor, sick, unworthy, or not educated enough to accomplish something, when in truth none of those things are real. They are excuses we have made up to hold ourselves back. I spent a year of training uncovering those limiting beliefs within myself in order to be a better servant to my clients and community.

It's about service. I believe that we are all one in the mind and spirit of God. Therefore, anything I can do to raise my own consciousness to a greater level of love and compassion raises the consciousness of everyone. I am also a teacher, both in the example I set with my own life and in the classroom where I teach spiritual principles and practices.

It's about commitment. I completed an extensive training program over four years to become a coach. I am committed to daily spiritual practice that includes prayer, meditation, journaling, reading spiritually-uplifting material, spontaneous living and service. I regularly use the services of my own spiritual living coach. My spiritual practice serves two purposes. One is to keep myself in the mindset of "I love my life!" The other is to keep myself in fit spiritual shape to serve my clients.

Why bother with a spiritual living coach? We work with the understanding that it is our consciousness—beliefs, thoughts and feelings—that create our experiences. The client generally comes to the session dissatisfied with some aspect of his or her life, and we determine what in the client needs to change to create the desired results. Typically the session begins with a peaceful centering, followed by a period of discussion relative to what the client wants to experience. There may be some client-participation activities—things he or she can do beyond the session to support the changes desired. Each session closes with prayer affirming the client's objective. Probably the best reason I can offer is for using a coach: it's a very good thing to talk regularly with someone who is not living inside your own head!

"It's the repetition of affirmations that leads to belief. And once that belief becomes a deep conviction, things begin to happen." Muhammad Ali

To Ponder: What is going on inside my head? Is it a scary place? Do I feel stuck? Held back? Empty? Dissatisfied? How might a coach be able to help?

Ponderings

Rudeness, Anger and Peace (A)

As this wonderful learning experience of life would have it, yesterday I wrote about not taking things personally. That was followed later in the day by a client coming into my workplace and being outright rude from the get-go. My job is tax preparation, so frustration among clients is common, but rudeness is not. Thus I had the perfect opportunity to practice not taking this personally.

I noted that this incident pushed my "self-righteous anger" button. This is an emotion I have loved in the past, probably to the point of addiction. "How dare she be so rude to me?!?!" and so on. My inner chatter was alternating between being snippy back at her and simply listening peacefully. I responded to her questions calmly. It helped that I had the figures handy to support my answers. She left, still ranting as she went out the door.

Her departing comments sealed the deal—this all had nothing to do with me (which I knew was true at the beginning). It was all about her life's frustrations. Therefore, why let all that mess, which I am clueless about anyway, disturb my own peace? One choice would have been to get all wound up in self-righteous anger, which may have given me a temporary rush, but would have left wasted energy and distress in its wake. I could have stooped to the client's level and been rude right back to her. However, I seek in life to lift my consciousness rather than lower it. Instead, I chose the peace of not taking her behavior personally. I went on about my business, had an enjoyable evening at home, and was left with another topic for this book. Her rudeness became my bonus, all for not taking it personally.

"As you make a habit of not taking anything personally, you won't need to place your trust in what others say or do. You will only need to trust yourself to make responsible choices. You are never responsible for the actions of others; you are only responsible for you." Don Miguel Ruiz

To Ponder: How do I respond when someone behaves rudely? Am I fond of being angry, especially self-righteous anger? What other choice(s) might I make in such a situation? How might a different choice affect me and my life?

Ponderings

Bravery (A)

This topic has as much potential as the number of stars in the sky, because bravery is a very personal thing. What is brave for one may be ordinary to another. For instance, for me, it was extremely brave to skydive. But that's often a once-in-a-lifetime brave. It has taken much more bravery for me to learn to say "no" when I truly want to say "no," to stand up for myself consistently, to buck the opinions of so-called "experts." Really, just living each day well on this amazing planet full of amazing humans is brave.

It's very brave for someone to cry in a public setting. Most folks don't want to be seen doing that. It's brave to let someone else know how you truly feel, and to express your needs. Any activity that involves heights and potentially falling requires great bravery. Driving in busy, congested traffic may be brave to some, or adventuring into new places. Admitting you don't know, and being willing to learn, is quite bold and courageous. Anyone who has taken on the job of parenting is brave.

Anyone who has ever lost a loved one is brave for moving through grief and continuing on with life. Certainly anyone who has ever had a life-threatening illness is powerfully brave. Watching your children learn life's tough lessons, and keeping "hands-off," qualifies as bravery. Every broken-heart survivor has been brave. And praise be to those who have bravely rescued another from injury or death.

So you see, bravery abounds, both around you and within you. Celebrate your bold, adventuresome, "I can do this!" spirit.

"It's amazing to allow yourself to dare your own authentic walk in this lifetime, to listen to the love within you more than your fear." Tama Kieves

To Ponder: Where, when, how in my life have I been brave? Note instances of bravery in my daily life. Celebrate my courage!

Ponderings

The Perfectly Good Airplane

On February 6, 2009, I mailed letters to 44 women I know in Wichita offering this opportunity:

What would you do if you weren't afraid?

What is the scariest thing you can think of? I'm not talking death of a loved one here. I'm talking for you, personally. For me it is jumping out of a perfectly good airplane.

So here's your chance to go on the adventure of a lifetime. This adventure covers all aspects of your being: physical, emotional, mental and spiritual. This is a completely personal commitment which will take you beyond the fears that have been holding you back, ones you may not even be aware of. There's always more to us than we know.

****

The group requirements were monthly meetings, coaching sessions, writing assignments, payment of $50 (half going into our adventure fund), and participation in assorted activities, such as the Kansas State University Challenge Course. The ultimate requirement was sky-diving. To be in the group, you had to have not sky-dived.

Five women plus myself answered this call of Spirit. I fondly refer to this as a "shove" of Spirit, as I tend to resist them and Spirit is relentless. I have had these shoves before and going with them has resulted in the best experiences of my life, so I knew that, despite my terror at the thought of jumping out of a perfectly good airplane, I had to form this group.

I was afraid even dropping the invitation letters into the mailbox. I did it anyway, with two thoughts: relief and perspective—those who aren't interested will not hesitate to pitch them. Those who are interested will be divinely drawn.

And so it was. We had our first meeting on April 5, 2009. We were a group of women who didn't know what we were getting into, but said "YES!" anyway. And a group of women who said, "Ah, June 26, 2010, is WAY far away." That's the date we chose for our sky-dive. We selected our name that first meeting—the Brave Broads.

From the start, the group wildly exceeded my expectations. I am proud of every one of us. We each held up our end of the bargain, contributing our money and committing the time to doing the coaching sessions, monthly meetings, activities and writing assignments. I saw us move through things that would have baffled and/or brought us down, release old beliefs and practices that no longer served us, and stand up for ourselves. We all became more confident, more appreciative of our gifts and strengths; more understanding of our shadows; more loving of the complete, unique wonderful package that each of us is. Most importantly, I saw us all practice and consistently use the skill of looking at things differently—change our thinking, change our lives—always for the better.

This was a divinely gathered, guided and guarded group. I had complete confidence from the beginning idea, that Spirit had my back, and our backs, throughout it all.

Days pass, as days will, and June 2010 arrived, and we all began to realize that June 26, our reserved sky-diving date, was just around the corner. Nervousness and angst built up throughout the month for all of us, even in our one Broad who initially said she wasn't afraid to sky-dive. We had a pre-dive party on Friday, June 25, sharing a meal and assorted activities to relieve the tension. We all left that party knowing that "We are going to do this. WE ARE BRAVE BROADS!"

Saturday, June 26, was the perfect day weather-wise for sky-diving (as I knew it would be). We arrived at 9:30 am at Air Capital Drop Zone and started with the "you could die" video and paperwork. Trust me, it was overkill (pun intended). We had brief training in how we would step out of the plane onto a step about 2' long and 10" wide. We practiced the position we needed to be in for free fall. Then it was time for the first two to harness up to go.

BB#1 and Martin, tandem instructor, went into the plane first, to come out second. I and Mark, tandem instructor, went into the plane last to come out first. Once the plane took off, the realization set in—this is it, I am not landing <u>in</u> the plane. On the 20-minute flight, I experienced tears of awe at how perfectly everything had flowed from the initial idea to the sky-dive. I eventually let go of my death grip on the wall of the plane. I enjoyed the beautiful Kansas landscape. Comically enough, as you are flying up to sky-dive, you have to wear a seatbelt. We flew up to 10,000 feet. Mark hooked himself to my back at the four corners of our torsos, and pulled the straps so tight, you couldn't have put a piece of tissue paper between us. That was comforting. The pilot gently lurched the plane giving the instructors the signal that it was time to go. Mark reminded me of the free fall position and opened the plane door. Even writing this now, I can feel it in my body. I have photos, and facial expressions don't lie, I was crazy scared.

We moved out onto the step as practiced, and upon the signal READY-SET-GO, rolled off the step. It was an instantaneous switch from complete terror to utter ecstasy. We were in free-fall for 30 seconds and 5,000 feet, as a smaller chute opened to slow us down. I am proud to say that I did not scream or cuss, and I did not even think to yell "pull the cord!" because the freefall was over so quickly. Mark opened the parachute, we were jerked upright, and it was an even more incredible joyride from then on. The parachutes are surprisingly steerable, and we leisurely floated over the Kansas countryside for about five minutes. I think I said "Oh, wow!" about 50 times on the way down, along with a few "I did it!" and "I feel like the Queen of the Universe!" We landed smoothly, easy, and gently as practiced to cheers and hugs. BB#1 and Martin touched down just a moment or two after us. It was AWESOME!

Every Broad completed the sky-dive successfully. If that day wasn't a miracle, I don't know what a miracle is. I am so profoundly grateful. The main lesson that I took from that experience is that the fear going into it was grossly out-of-proportion to the actual event. I would venture that this is true for probably 99.9% of our fears. Each of us truly earned the title, and will always be, a Brave Broad.

Viewing Death as Birth (W)

Sometimes we hear or read something we already know, but in an extra-receptive state, it really sinks into us in a much more meaningful way. My mother-in-law doesn't get upset when someone passes, no matter how close the relationship. I've found this interesting. Recently she said that she doesn't understand why people get upset when someone one dies; the person has gone on to a good place, and they are missed, yes, but there's no need to be sad for them. I believe this, and it was good to hear her perspective.

What if we view death as another birth process? I believe life is eternal, that we existed somewhere and somehow even before conception, and we continue forever. So we are continually being birthed into another experience. Our live birth process here on earth, in any species, is really quite phenomenal. Then when it is time to leave, we let go of this body and are born into the next experience. Could we celebrate the birthing at death the way we celebrate a newborn? I believe in some dimension that the celebration is just as grand.

A fundamental condition of life on Earth is free will. I believe on some level that we each make the choice of when to arrive and when to leave, whether it is conscious or unconscious. A fundamental aspect of that free will thing is that no one wants anyone else messing with his or her right to choose. This brings us to what is commonly called suicide—the conscious decision and action to move from this life to the next. This is not a sin, as so many human-created religions would have one believe. It is a use of the free will we all have. It can be horribly painful for those left behind, but it is a release into goodness for the person who makes the choice to finish life here. It is grand for the person to be free of a life that was simply not working for them. We are held in love eternally, everywhere we exist, in whatever form. Holding this belief enables us to gradually chip away at the trauma of death and celebrate it as another in a line of many rebirths.

"The destination is a happy life, an accomplished life, that doesn't end with death but with eternal life." Angelo Scola

To Ponder: What are my beliefs surrounding death? Are they comforting? If not, what are other possibilities relative to my understanding of death?

Ponderings

Self-Forgiveness (A)

It is this simple: the person I need to forgive the most, and the one least likely to be forgiven, is myself. True for me, true for you. No harsher judgment exists than that which we lay upon ourselves. With so many self-imposed convictions of inadequacies and screw-ups, how can we ever begin to forgive ourselves?

Let's start with thought. You and only you control your thinking, and yes, you can guide it to a more uplifting pattern. The place to start is noticing what you are telling yourself, and when the criticism starts to flow, gently stop it and replace it with a better-feeling thought. Here's an example: "I totally screwed that up. I'm so stupid." vs. "I messed that up, but I was able to fix the problem, and I learned something from it." Those two thoughts feel very different, unforgiving vs. gentle kindness.

Note that each of us arrived here without an instruction book. We are ALL learning life via trial and error. We do dumb stuff. We don't do stuff we could have done. We utter words before we've truly engaged our brains. We say "yes" when we mean "no," and vice versa. We don't always put our best selves forward. No matter how perfect we may attempt to be, we are not. If we can't forgive ourselves, it is nearly impossible to forgive others.

Be your own best friend. You wouldn't brow-beat a friend who messed up, so don't whip yourself. Reach for that better-feeling thought and do it over and over. Make amends when needed—this is a powerful process in a loving self-care practice. Take breaks to breathe deeply and find one thing to appreciate about yourself. Let mistakes go. No one needs the extra weight of dragging those around. Focus more on what you do right rather than on what you do wrong. Treat yourself regularly to a pleasurable experience like a massage or pedicure. As we learn that we are worthy of loving, gentle care and make that a habit, self-forgiveness becomes a simple and routine process.

"Once you forgive yourself, the self-rejection in your mind is over. Self-acceptance begins, and the self-love will grow so strong that you will finally accept yourself just the way you are. That's the beginning of the free human. Forgiveness is the key." Miguel Angel Ruiz

To Ponder: Am I quite harsh with myself? Why? Let it out here. Observe my self-critical thoughts. How can I begin to reframe those to something more positive? Name one thing I appreciate about myself. Complete this sentence, "I forgive myself for _____."

Ponderings

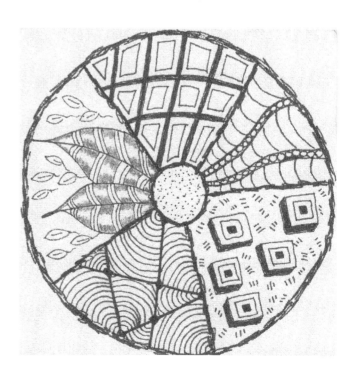

Patience (O)

Patience is defined as the capacity to accept or tolerate delay, trouble or suffering without getting angry or upset. In our instant-gratification world, it seems to be in short supply. I would offer that patience is the capacity to remain peaceful as the good in life unfolds without having to force or rush the process, knowing that there is a bigger picture that we rarely can see.

We practice patience frequently throughout a typical day, with our children, spouse, co-workers, service folks, other drivers. Sometimes we display lots of patience, sometimes, not so much. Next time you are feeling impatient, take note of how it feels in your body. I'd suggest that patience feels much better, and it is worth the effort to maintain that physical calm.

Then there is the more long-term patience. I have learned in my life that future changes start with spiritual nudges many weeks or months before changes actually happen. For instance, I am now being nudged to consider dropping some things from my weekly schedule. Just a few months ago, I would not have even considered such a thing. I have no idea what lies ahead that would make such a change worthwhile. I have learned to be patient, and simply curious, in these situations, knowing that if the nudges are there, new good is ramping up to manifest for me.

One of the circumstances that most challenges my patience is physical healing. You may have noted that a simple cut on your finger heals itself in its own good time, not instantaneously as we might like. Our bodies have an amazing capacity to heal if we support that process with our patience and self-care. Our bodies will take whatever time is needed to heal properly.

Patience and faith go hand in hand. Practicing either one enhances the other.

"It does not astonish or make us angry that it takes a whole year to bring into the house three great white peonies and two pale blue iris." May Sarton

To Ponder: Am I impatient? How is that serving me? Note instances throughout the day when I have practiced patience. Celebrate those. Am I feeling any nudges or pulls to make changes in my life? Can I be curious and patient and see where those take me?

Ponderings

This, Too, Shall Pass (O)

This commonly-heard phrase can truly be a sanity-saver. It reminds us that nothing ever stays the same. No matter how tough a current situation may seem, no matter how mired in mess we may feel, it will morph into a different experience. Thank the heavens!

This phrase is one of the popular slogans of recovery in 12-step programs. In those programs, it is used to remind the addict that the compelling urge to use will pass if it is not indulged. You don't need to be an addict to find it useful to wait for an urge to pass. For instance, it is handy in shopping or sticking with a commitment to a dietary or exercise plan.

One of the ways I use this phrase is in decision-making. I ask for support from my higher power to increase my desire, if a decision is in my best interests, or to let the desire pass if the decision is not for my highest good. This process has often enabled me to let go of "good" and allow something "even better" to come forth in my life.

A time of heavy grief also brings this phrase to mind. When we are grieving a great loss, possibly a loved one, or a job, or a physical setback, it seems like the misery will never lift, that it will go on forever. We humans are adaptable creatures, however. We deal with the situation, and life eventually moves us forward with a renewed outlook.

"This, too, shall pass" is also supportive of our patience practice. If the line is too long and moving too slow, if traffic is backed up, if flights are delayed—the endless annoyances of daily living—we can choose to be anxious or to let it go, allowing the annoyance to pass. Difficulties pass more quickly if we release them rather than hang on and stew in them.

"My current situation is not my final destination." Anonymous

To Ponder: What difficulties have I passed through in my life? Celebrate my ability to move forward. What is currently on my "annoyance" list? Can I see a way to release those and let them pass?

Ponderings

Hungry Heart (W)

Topics for this book have come to me in the most serendipitous ways. Leaving the pool area at the YMCA yesterday, I heard Bruce Springsteen's song with the lyrics, "Everybody's got a hungry heart, lay down your money and you play your part." I woke up planning to write about that, and this is the "Note from the Universe" (by Mike Dooley) I received this morning in my inbox:

> **"If you could actually stand in someone else's shoes to hear what they hear, see what they see, and feel what they feel, you would honestly wonder what planet they live on and be totally blown away by how different their 'reality' is from yours. You'd also never, in a million years, be quick to judge again."**

Springsteen's lyric is a quite profound spiritual statement. I believe we all come from, and eventually return to, a place of pure, unending bliss, and while here in human form, there's a part of us continually hungering to return to that state. It's a hunger that we spend our lifetimes trying to satisfy. We invest our life energy ("lay down your money") and live out our unique expression ("you play your part"). There are infinite routes folks take to sate the hunger, plenty of which are not socially acceptable or pleasing to those around them. Ultimately, however, everyone is working on his or her hungry heart. This all lends itself to the practice of loving and gentle compassion.

In the intense grieving period right after my dad returned to his bliss state, I realized that, since I wasn't wearing black clothing and a sign that said, "just lost my dad," no strangers knew the situation. How many folks was I encountering in a day who had just had a traumatic experience? It led me to practice kindness more intentionally, because we just don't know another's situation. "Everybody's got a hungry heart."

"Whether one believes in a religion or not, and whether one believes in rebirth or not, there isn't anyone who doesn't appreciate kindness and compassion." Dalai Lama

To Ponder: Re-reading the quote above, how can I apply that wisdom and practice more compassion in my life?

Ponderings

Why Not Smile (O/A)

I daresay that every single human being is even more beautiful when he or she is smiling. I can't think of anything more universally joy-inspiring than a baby's totally uninhibited grin. We <u>love</u> smiling, so why not do it, a lot?

The first place to use your smile is at yourself, in the mirror, in the morning, in all your bedhead, bleary-eyed glory. Give yourself a big "I love you!" grin. Why not?

It's a very fun experiment to smile and greet folks you pass on the street. Some ignore you, some are surprised and respond in kind, some even look at you like you are nuts. It's great entertainment. Best of all, you feel good because you've been friendly.

Wouldn't you like it if folks said your neighborhood or city is a friendly place to visit or live? Don't you want people to feel good when they are in your place of business? Smiling is at the root of that. It is a statement of welcome and openness to sharing the good around you.

One never knows how a simple smile can affect another. It may just be the thing they need to keep moving through a rough day. A smile can say "I believe in you" at a critical moment in someone's life.

Smiling feels good. I especially make the effort to smile at the grocery store and the gym, both places where folks may not necessarily want to be. Life is really good, and I want my personal presence to radiate that, and my smile is a handy way to accomplish it.

Smiling doesn't cost you anything. It can re-orient your attitude about your own life. It sets a great example for those around you. So why not smile?

"A smile is the light in your window that tells others that there is a caring, sharing person inside." Denis Waitley

To Ponder: Pay attention to how often I smile in a day. Can I add more smiles? Notice other people smiling at me. How does that feel? Note a time when a smile has been especially meaningful to me.

Ponderings

IMAGE (W)

Here's your chance to change how you consider this word forever. Our self-image is one of our most important and fundamental characteristics, because it reflects the summation of our beliefs. How about this: I'm a God expression. That's the truth. However, if the term "God" is not a pleasant or meaningful term to you, here are some other possibilities:

I'm a great experience.

I'm a glorious energizer.

I'm a generous embracer (I give great hugs).

I'm a genius employee.

I'm a gregarious enthusiast.

You get the idea and you can easily create your own image saying. You can google "words that start with the letter _" to spark your creativity and uniquely express your image.

The key point in all this is that "I am" statements are creative, so pay attention to what image you choose. Make sure it fits comfortably, uplifts you and is easy to remember and repeat often.

"The 'self-image' is the key to human personality and human behavior. Change the self image and you change the personality and the behavior." Maxwell Maltz

To Ponder: What is my IMAGE statement that brings out my best, most vibrant self? Repeat it often with enthusiasm. Note how it feels in my body. Note how it affects my daily living.

Ponderings

Always Do Your Best (A)

This is the fourth of the Four Agreements from the book of that name by Don Miguel Ruiz.

Always do your best. It sounds like being perfect, doesn't it? It's a far cry from that, however. There are several key points about this Agreement. The first is that your best changes constantly. Your best is one way when you awaken in the morning, refreshed, and another way when you are tired at the end of a long workday. Your best also changes over time as you evolve. Doing your best is one way that you express your own unique talents and abilities.

Your best also relates directly to what you are doing. If you are doing something for a reward, for instance, working only for the paycheck, it's not likely you'll enjoy what you do, and not likely you'll even attempt to do your best. But if you are engaged in something you love, doing your best becomes much easier.

Doing your best has a super side-benefit. Having done your best, if your internal critic attempts to judge your efforts, you can respond, "I did my best." That shuts down the inner critic with the truth.

How is doing your best not perfectionism? You do your best because you want to, not to please your inner critic or someone else. Perfectionism always involves the desire to please. Doing your best pleases you, and makes you happy, and that truly is all that matters. You cannot affect others' happiness.

All Four Agreements require practice, practice, practice. Your happiness depends upon it.

"Taking action is being alive. It's taking the risk to go out and express your dream." Don Miguel Ruiz

To Ponder: Take a situation and consider what "doing my best" means. Am I trying to please my inner critic or someone other than myself? Am I spending my time doing what I love to do? How can I incorporate more of "doing my best" into my life?

Ponderings

Generosity (A)

The first person who comes to mind when I think of generosity is my dad. I learned how to practice it from him. He gave money easily to those causes he deemed worthwhile, and gave of his time collecting in our countryside for such things as the American Cancer Society. He talked often about how the Miller family was blessed, and it was the right thing to do, to share our blessings. He was always exceedingly generous with his family.

Stephen G. Post is a professor of preventive medicine at Stony Brook University. In his book, *Why Good Things Happen to Good People*, Post wrote, "The startling findings from our many studies demonstrate that if you engage in helping activities as a teen, you will still be reaping health benefits 60 or 70 years later. Generous behavior is closely associated with reduced risk of illness and mortality and lower rates of depression."

A key element of generosity is giving freely with no expectation of return or reward. We practice generosity simply for the joy of being helpful. It's giving because you <u>want</u> to give, not because you are feeling pressured or told you "should." Giving under pressure, from yourself or others, is not generosity.

Why aren't we more generous? The main reason is fear of not having enough for ourselves, especially enough money or time. Some rebel against religious upbringings where they were nagged incessantly to give. Others are suspicious as to whether their funds will be used effectively.

It's common to think of generosity in terms of money, but it is much more than that. We have many valuable "commodities" to share such as our time, a listening ear, useful skills, or handy tools. We all have more to share than we realize.

"True generosity is an offering; given freely and out of pure love. No strings attached. No expectations. Time and love are the most valuable possession you can share." Suze Orman

To Ponder: What do I have to offer? How do I currently practice generosity? How might I be more generous? Whom would I like to help?

Ponderings

Good or Bad (W)

It is an extremely prevalent behavior among human to immediately evaluate a person, place or situation as "good" or "bad." This is black-and-white thinking that is based in the very ancient part of our brains. It is also widely supported by our culture.

As we evolve as humans and learn to use the more advanced part of our brains, we begin to explore and consider these rapid good-bad judgments. For one thing, we can never see the whole big picture. We don't know another person fully, and we can't see all parts of a situation clearly. Also, time has a way of tempering the good-bad evaluation.

Here are some examples. An addict recognizes her problem, seeks and embraces recovery, and lives a joyful, productive life. Was the addiction good or bad? A serious illness causes a man to change his eating habits and start exercising to be more healthy. Was the illness good or bad? A homosexual person in an unhappy marriage "comes out," breaks up the marriage, and both spouses go on to new, happy relationships. Was the coming out good or bad?

There is often some bit of bad in a good situation (a fabulous vacation comes to an end) and some measure of good in a bad situation (pain often incites change). In the midst of a tough situation, when it's hard to see any good, it is useful to affirm: I know there is good in this, and I am capable of finding it. It takes the sting out of a difficult situation if we can hold onto the idea that there is good in it somewhere. Ultimately, it is acceptance of our experiences without judgment that leads to peace.

"As soon as you concern yourself with the 'good' and 'bad' of your fellows, you create an opening in your heart for maliciousness to enter. Testing, competing with, and criticizing others weaken and defeat you." Morihei Ueshiba

To Ponder: Notice my tendency to apply labels of "good" and "bad." Can I step back and see the possibility of both in a situation? What if I don't label the person or situation?

Ponderings

Forgiveness of Others (A)

This is not my favorite subject. Forgiveness of others can be challenging and seemingly unending work. First you have to develop the desire and willingness to forgive and then actually do it. The deeper the perceived wound, the more onerous the task of forgiveness seems.

Why forgive? "That as$$#(*hole did me wrong, he is the one at fault, he should apologize, I didn't do anything wrong, I don't deserve this." That in a nutshell is our typical resistance to forgiveness. It feels like we are letting the offender off the hook. Alas, we can be fairly certain that the offender isn't disturbed. We are the ones assuming the victim mentality, carrying around the angst, and keeping ourselves off-center and distressed. We forgive for our own benefit, not for the good of the offender.

Anyone who inspires any sort of negative emotional charge within us is someone to forgive. We may find ourselves forgiving certain folks on a regular basis. In fact, it's an excellent practice before bedtime to look through your day and forgive as needed, so that you don't carry angst into your sleep time.

One way to approach forgiveness is the idea that everything happens <u>for</u> me, rather than everything happens <u>to</u> me. People are in our lives for a reason; there are no accidents. If we can find the blessing in an ugly situation, forgiveness becomes easier. There is a story elsewhere in this book called **Ken, My Greatest Teacher** (p. 88). It's a tale of lifelong abuse and powerful learning, and yes, forgiveness.

An extremely effective method of forgiveness comes from the 12-step programs. For the person you want to forgive, pray every day for two weeks that they experience all the good you would have in your own life. It works, because prayer changes the one praying, the objective of forgiveness.

It <u>is</u> possible, through expanding self-knowledge and trust, to live in such a manner that very little upsets you, and therefore, forgiveness is rarely needed. A lofty goal, indeed, but possible through dedicated spiritual practice.

"Judgment and love are opposites. From one come all the sorrows of the world. But from the other comes the peace of God." A Course in Miracles

To Ponder: Whom do I need to forgive for my own peace? Use the 2-week prayer method, or write them a forgiveness letter (don't send it). Describe the results. Repeat as needed.

Ponderings

Our Innate Ability to Heal (H)

This topic is not about natural remedies or natural healing modalities; rather it is about how amazing and intelligent our bodies are. We need look no further than a woman's ability to take two tiny cells, sperm and ovum, and turn that into another human being, to see how incredible the human body is.

Equally amazing, though rather taken for granted, is the body's ability to heal a wound or repair a broken bone. We don't consciously make that happen. The body is always working at keeping itself healthy and doing repairs as needed.

The body is energy in motion. Even at the most restful states, there is a flurry of activity going on in every cell. You are breathing, your heart is beating, blood is flowing everywhere, and tiny amounts of hormones are regulating a multitude of functions. I tell my yoga students who experience some soreness the day after doing a new pose that it is "energy moving in places it was not moving before, and that's a good thing."

I would offer that it takes the body some amount of energy to heal, the more severe the injury, illness or surgery, the more energy it takes. This is why we want to rest when we are healing, to direct the energy to restoration rather than all those other things we think we should be doing. Folks rarely give their bodies the rest time needed to heal. We're too impatient. Our bodies do have the means, however, to slow us down if necessary for our best healthy balance.

Lastly, our bodies do respond to the body talk and thoughts we direct at them. Words of loving-kindness are supportive of health and help the body function at its optimum level. Words of criticism and negativity have the opposite effect. We choose how we address our body, and we can change it from negative to positive. Appreciating the magnificent body you live in is yet another rewarding spiritual practice.

"You can't afford to get sick, and you can't depend on the present health-care system to keep you well. It's up to you to protect and maintain your body's innate capacity for health and healing by making the right choices in how you live." Andrew Weil

To Ponder: Select one thing right now to appreciate about my body. Consider how amazing it is. What if I didn't have that item or function? Each day, choose another body part or function and give it loving-kindness and appreciation throughout the day. How is my attitude about my body changing?

Ponderings

Honoring a Place of Grace

"When you truly awake spiritually, you realize you are caged. You wake up and realize that you can hardly move in there. You're constantly hitting the limits of your comfort zone. You see that you're afraid to tell people what you really think. You see that you're too self-conscious to freely express yourself. You see that you have to stay on top of everything in order to be okay.

Why? There's really no reason. You have set these limits on yourself. If you don't stay within them, you get scared, you feel hurt, and you feel threatened. That's your cage. The tiger knows the limits of his cage when he hits the bars. You know the limits of your cage when the psyche starts to resist. Your bars are the outer boundary of your comfort zone. The minute you come to the edge of your cage, it lets you know it in no uncertain terms."
Michael A. Singer

****

My dad taught me to swim at Whipples Dam State Park in central Pennsylvania when I was a little girl of age six or seven. He later built a 20'x40' concrete swimming pool at our house, and spent many hours maintaining it, though he rarely went in it. That was true love, albeit with considerable nagging from my mom.

I've been a swimmer most of my life. I love to swim, and I love being in the water. I'm in my early 60s and I can swim a mile, no problem.

Recovering from an extremely painful back injury in 1996, I committed to swimming regularly, and I have swum over 100 miles every year since 1998. Being the nerd I am, the lap counts are all recorded in a spreadsheet. That's basically three times a week all year long, and I've visited YMCAs all over the country to keep up my swim routine. When the kids were little, my husband and I alternated mornings at the Y. Taking turns at workouts was a powerful motivator, because if I didn't go, there were no make-ups, and I didn't get to go again for two more days.

Swimming laps uses me on all levels—physical obviously—but it's also meditation time for me, an opportunity to release emotional energy, and a time of great creativity and idea-gathering.

A few years ago, the Universe gave me a new method for swimming. An acquaintance working in the same office building downtown offered me an instructional DVD of the Auburn swim team. He said it had helped him swim more efficiently. Applying the methods shown on the DVD, along with seeing how Michael Phelps does the backstroke, has completely changed how I swim. It is much more efficient and feels very natural.

I am often complimented by other swimmers, mostly saying "You make it look easy." It is easy. I've shown several people the method, and I love to help them when asked. I'm not a fast swimmer by any means. I'm built for endurance, not speed, and this is evident in many aspects of my life.

Lap swimming is the one place where I feel graceful. It's a place where I feel free of "my weight problem." My body feels expansive, yet light, and I love how I feel when I'm swimming.

A few years ago, a friend gave me the idea of wearing a unitard for swimming. I guess I'd seen them, but never thought of buying one. I looked into them—they are made of polyester, a long-lasting material for frequent chlorine dunks, and they are much less expensive than regular swimsuits. Perfect! I ordered one, getting a conservative blue color.

I'm the only person I've ever seen wearing one at the Y.

Enter my critical inner roommate: "This is weird. No one else wears one. People don't mention it, like it's too weird to comment on. You are large."

Shutting up the inner roommate, I love to swim in it. It fits great, covers more than a regular swimsuit, and I love how I feel moving through the water in it.

The time came to re-order another unitard. I really wanted a red one, red being my favorite color. Enter my inner roommate: "You will look like a giant tomato."

One of the things my life-long overweight status has done for me is to get me out of the cage aspect of what folks think of me. It's been an issue all my life, but it hasn't kept me from doing the things I want to do, i.e., my body will never be a "model's body," so I really don't care any more what others think of it. Any vestiges of that mentality were eliminated in my Forrest Yoga teacher training. I haven't limited myself by "when I lose weight…" I am extraordinarily appreciative of all the things my body can do.

I ordered the red suit…

The first day I wore it, the female lifeguard walked by my lane as I was using the kickboard, and I said, "Good morning!" and she said, "Good morning, I like your red suit."

The second time I wore it, after swimming, there was only one other woman in the locker room, and she asked me where I got my suit, saying, "I really like it. I want something that stays put on me." I gave her all the details.

The third time I wore it, I was swimming late morning, a very unusual time for me to be there. When I finished, another woman in the pool asked me about the way I swim. It turns out she has neck surgery-shoulder-scoliosis issues, and she said, "The way you swim, it looks like it doesn't hurt." Off we went from there…

I'd say the red suit is a noticeable "hit!"

Put Down the Phone (A)

Whatever device it is that you are incessantly attached to, put it down. Let go of it for a bit. This action won't kill you, I promise.

I am as guilty as anyone about being attached to my phone. It's my calendar, guidance system, connection to a lot of folks, time piece and sports reporter, as well as my phone. It's an extremely useful tool in one very small unit.

One day not long ago I accidently left my phone at home when I left for work. I went through the whole day without it. Although I habitually kept reaching for it and looking for it, I really was fine without it.

Scientists are noting two particularly unfortunate side effects of extensive cell phone usage—prolonged sitting and negative effects on mental fitness. "Sitting is the new smoking" is the phrase used to describe the deleterious effect on our bodies of sitting for long periods. Extensive sitting is linked to loads of diseases. Our bodies are designed to move, not sit for hours and hours. We tend to be sitting most of the time we are using our phones, an unhealthy combination.

The other side effect of cell phone usage is a negative effect on mental fitness. We used to figure our route by reading paper maps, use our alphabetizing skills to look up words in the dictionary, and recall facts and important numbers from memory. Depending on our hand-held device for such things means we aren't exercising our brains, and brain exercise is just as important to a long and happy life as is physical exercise. The brain grows stronger through use, just like our muscles, and it develops new neural pathways as a result of stimulation. The brain literally shrinks from lack of stimulation.

So put down the phone, get up and move, and use your brain. Go outside, breathe and stretch. Go through the alphabet and list one thing for each letter that makes you smile. Life can be more relaxed and at the same time, invigorating for both body and mind. Put down the phone.

"The cell phone has become the adult's transitional object, replacing the toddler's teddy bear for comfort and a sense of belonging." Margaret Heffernan

To Ponder: How much time do I spend using my phone or other electronic devices? Limit checking email, messages, etc. to twice a day at specific times. How does that feel? Practice letting go.

Ponderings

Completion (A)

While I don't know at this moment where this writing lands in the book, this is the last of the 122 "ponder sets" to be written. Certainly the book is far from complete, but this is a huge milestone in the lengthy process of creating a book.

My general impression of would-be writers is that they think <u>writing</u> the book is the tough part. That's not the case for me. It's a matter of some discipline to make myself write nearly every day. One of the things I learned about myself in this writing process is that the act of writing is a spiritual practice for me, an essential connection to my Higher Power that is very life-supporting. I tend to get very cranky without it.

I was given a very clear picture of what the finished product of this book looks like. There is much work to be done to get this rough draft into that form. The Universe, I know, is already lining up people and resources for me to easily create that vision.

What I suggest is the tough part of any project is releasing it to the public, letting it go. Once it is "out there," there is no taking it back for one more tweak. It's open to criticism. What if no one is interested? You've poured heart and soul into this, and what if it's a flop? The reason I can write about this is because I've been through it with my first book. Ultimately, no one was interested, and yet, here I am, I lived to tell about it and eventually write another book. However, I am quite different this time around.

Spirit has been nudging me for years to write another book. I've resisted for years. Finally, my experience in a deep meditative moment while on retreat convinced me to go for it. I wrote this for myself, for the pleasure and challenge of doing it, and I have no expectations relative to what happens when it is ultimately finished. I'm not emotionally invested in where it goes. I know I'll continue to live a charmed life no matter what unfolds with this book.

I am also more open to asking for help. That is huge progress for me, and quite necessary to turn this very rough draft into the finished product I envisioned and which you are now holding. It is also way more fun to write and create without the pressure of needing to be a success. I enjoy the process. Isn't that what all of life is supposed to be about?

"People who live their dreams have big, wide-open hearts and the rapier focus of a secret agent on a precarious mission. They do not sweat in heat. They do not run because of a tabby cat's shadow in the alley. They no longer fear disappointment or disruption. They meet uncertainty with certainty. They keep moving in the direction of their dreams and they don't turn back. It's a constant redirection of the mind. And it works." Tama Kieves

To Ponder: What do I want to create? Take one baby step and enjoy it. Repeat.

Ponderings

You Are It (W)

These words of wisdom are from Emma Curtis Hopkins: **"No word can express your understanding of God. You are it."** Regardless of whether you commonly use the term "God," you are an emanation of universal energy, and how you live and move as it is a reflection of your understanding of your true nature.

Below are some adjective pairs describing "ends of the spectrum" human characteristics.

loving - fearful

joyful - depressed

expansive - limited

creative - bored

inclusive - exclusive

grateful - lacking

energized - weary

powerful - weak

kind - cruel

complete - inadequate

confident - insecure

generous - hoarding

all-knowing - confused

focused - inattentive

peaceful - anxious

None of us is consistently at either end of the spectrum all the time. We waver between the ends a lot. I was raised in a religion that led me to believe that God was on the left of the list, and humans were pretty much hanging to the right. I have, via my ongoing spiritual practice, realized that we are all on the left—that those qualities are our true nature—and we can lean toward that side if we choose. That's Hopkins' point… we are continually expressing our understanding of who we really are. Our "walk" says everything about what we believe, no matter what our "talk" is.

"Where can we go to find God if we cannot see Him in our own hearts and in every living being." Swami Vivekananda

To Ponder: Looking at the list above, where on the spectrum does my behavior generally show up? How is that serving me? How does that reflect my understanding of God or my higher self? What sort of internal changes could move me more to the left on the spectrum?

Ponderings

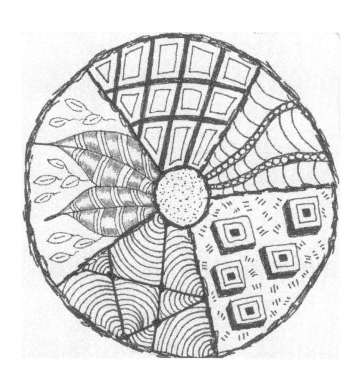

What's Next? (W)

You've spent some valuable life time exploring who you are, what you believe and how you express yourself in the world. You've learned quite a bit.

Your first mission is to celebrate. Look back over the book and notice what you've delved into and what you've discovered. Appreciate that you've been brave enough to journey within. Observe what actions have made life better for you, and…

Practice. Practice. Practice. Many ideas presented here are lifelong practices to use on a regular basis to stay centered in <u>w</u>holeness. Your overall <u>h</u>ealth depends on your being <u>o</u>pen to new ideas and experiences, and repeating those <u>a</u>ctions that make you feel good, both in the moment and over time. Make a daily commitment to loving self-care.

You know what to do, and when and how to do it. You have nurtured a trust in your inner wisdom that will take you to great new adventures, your adventures. Enjoy the journey!

"The joy of life comes from our encounters with new experiences, and hence there is no greater joy than to have an endlessly changing horizon, for each day to have a new and different sun." Christopher McCandless

To Ponder: My celebrations? My best practices? My adventures?

Ponderings

ABOUT THE AUTHOR

Leta Miller is lovin' life and spreadin' joy, using her talents to bring people together and inspire them to love who they are and to be the best that they can be.

Leta's many roles include author, spiritual life coach, creator, yoga teacher, wife, mother, organizer, world traveler, recovering addict, golfer, retreat leader, tax preparer, domestic goddess, athlete, fanatic Cubs fan and budding artist. She lives in Wichita, Kansas, with her husband of 30+ years, Dennis Hardin.

Leta's event schedule and more of her writings are located at the Brave Broad Blog (thebravebroad.blogspot.com).

Made in the USA
Lexington, KY
28 October 2017